KINGDOM ALIGNMENT

An Illumination of the King

ENDORSEMENTS

Written with prophetic insight and an artist's dramatic flair, this outstanding book by Prophetess Lora Allison is a book for all believers... and risk takers.

What Lora urges us on to is true Kingdom life, devoid of pretense, filled with adventure. We are called as God's chosen and royal people towards a life of abandonment to God's Kingdom. This Kingdom, not physical but visible in manifestation, inaugurated by Christ and ever expanding, is the only place to dwell if we are to achieve our divine purpose.

I encourage you to prepare your heart for the journey found in this warm and wonderful work.

Dr. Stan DeKoven, President
Vision International University

We are coming into a glorious age -- an age when God has chosen to unfold to His Body fresh understanding of the magnificent Kingdom of God. Several years ago God used Lora in my life to challenge me to investigate and study the Kingdom. It has been the most revelatory journey of my 37 years of Christian ministry.

Now you too can embark on the Kingdom journey with her through her newest book. It is thorough and filled with insight that will be life changing. What she writes on Kingdom alignment alone is transforming. You will never know your assignments from God until you are in proper alignment.

I know this lady, I'd read anything she writes. This one is her best: don't miss its truth.

Bob L. Phillips
Senior Pastor of Encourager Church, Houston, Texas
Co-Founder of The Kairos Journal

Wow! As one who writes and teaches others to write books, I'm captivated by this book. The highest commendation I can offer is this: I want everyone I love to read this book! It's a treasure trove for the believer.

Lora, thank you for your life of integrity, passion for the Son of God, and balance in practice. Your Godly wisdom is refreshing to read. As your brother in Christ, fellow minister, and fellow Houstonian, who's known and admired you for years, I couldn't be more honored than to commend this excellent resource!

Eddie Smith, Best selling Author and Speaker
www.EddieAndAlice.com

Lora's book is for a time such as this! Researchers inform us that only 9% of the Church in America has a Biblical world-view, or a clear understanding of the revelation of the Kingdom of God. There are a number of books on *Kingdom* and some on *alignment*, but none that I know of that connect and relate both as Lora has done for us.

This book clearly instructs us that Kingdom advancement is directly related to the proper alignment of our lives and ministries. I especially appreciate her insight on aligning genders and generations so the purposes of God can be fulfilled in the Body of Christ and in the nations! Use this volume for personal edification and for teaching others.

Jim Hodges, Founder and President
Federation of Ministers and Churches International

Awesome! Lora Allison's book *Kingdom Alignment* takes us to a whole new level of revelatory insight! This message of the Kingdom is vital to the time in which we live. Lora has the ability to help you navigate into the supernatural as well as to apply Kingdom reality to everyday life.

This book is brilliantly filled with deep truths and personal insights that will enable you to become *aligned* and to see more clearly. If you desire to experience the Kingdom operating in greater measure in your life and in your world, then this book is a must read.

Dr. Kluane Spake, Apostle, Author, Speaker
www.kluane.org

Lora, a uniquely gifted communicator, does not merely give us a visual of possibility, but through her own crucibles of experience gives us insight and revelation of what should be. She reminds us that we cannot build upon cracked or faulty foundations if we are to have proper Kingdom Authority or Influence.

This book will help the reader to understand that with proper foundations laid with sacrifices made, we can build on The Kingdom that never fails. Through proper Alignments, Associations, Agreements and Attitudes, we will then have authentic Kingdom Authority and influence.

The late Edwin Louis Cole taught me that "The characteristics of the Kingdom emanate from the characteristics of the King." We are in the cusp of historical transitions and if we are to have lasting impact, we must take to heart the principles laid out in this book.

Doug Stringer
Founder, Somebody Cares America/International
Founder, Turning Point Ministries International

Lora Allison is one of God's treasures. She has opened our hearts to see and understand in a realm that few understand today. This book will cause your heart to sing and deepen your heart to know and worship our King.

Cindy Jacobs
Generals.International

God has an army that is aligning, advancing, and displaying His Kingdom power. In Kingdom Alignment, Lora Allison captures the culture, administration, and operation of a Kingdom that is beyond the natural rule. Lora also captures and expresses how the heart of the King rules His subjects.

Kingdom Alignment helps you understand how and why the Lord is snapping you into place. His alignment is producing a holy array and order that will change the course of the world. If you are a believer and the Kingdom of God is within you, Kingdom Alignment will help you see into a realm beyond where you presently live and operate.

Chuck D. Pierce
President, Global Spheres Inc.
President, Glory of Zion International
Harvest Watchman, Global Harvest Ministries

KINGDOM ALIGNMENT

AN ILLUMINATION OF THE KING

LORA ALLISON

Intermedia Publishing Group

KINGDOM ALIGNMENT
An Illumination of the King

Published by:
Intermedia Publishing Group, Inc.
P.O. Box 2825
Peoria, Arizona 85380
www.intermediapub.com

ISBN 978-1-935529-27-9

Printed in the United States of America by Epic Print Solutions

CONTENTS

PREFACE

Kingdom Alignment is a prophetic book, encompassing unique literary styles and allegory in addition to strong practical sections which bring clear definition in areas of daily life in the Kingdom. Woven into this book are pertinent sections from previous works of the author which have direct bearing and emphasis as we consider the subject of alignment in the Kingdom of God.

This is a book which seeks to give overall vision of the Kingdom from the heart of the King. Knowing His heart and nature is a key component for Kingdom alignment as we also speak of governmental issues and structures often bringing confusion or division in this season of changing church perspectives.

May the Lord give us fresh impartation of the Spirit of wisdom and revelation in this crucial and strategic season in the Body of Christ. Our desire in this hour is to hear clearly the direction of our God and to obey whatever the cost, that we may continue to have a clear and vital part in the carrying out of His purposes in the earth.

> And this gospel of the kingdom will be preached in all the world as a witness to all the nations, and then the end will come.
>
> Matthew 24:14, NKJV

ACKNOWLEDGEMENTS

My heart is full of gratitude for the rich treasures the Lord has placed in my life in the relationships of family, friends, and ministry associates across the world. You have enriched my life beyond measure, and made me more than who I am.

What joy it is to have the support of family! My wonderful, unique, witty and intelligent husband, Dr. Richard Allison, has supported me, prayed for me, and endured, to date, the writing of seven books. Truly, his rewards will be rich in heaven: a college professor/engineer married to a prophetic, artist, musician, woman minister. Just think about it! It will make you pray for him diligently. Thank you, Richard, for everything.

Also in the treasure chest of my life are so many staff, friends, and intercessors who have literally kept me alive, healthy, and sane while I juggle numerous balls at once, in various places in the world. To all of you my heartfelt thanks for going to bat for me in the spiritual realm, and also in the shark-infested, dog-eat-dog world around us. Thank you for supporting, loving, and praying for me in the midst of it all. I would not begin to name you, you definitely know who you are. My love and thanks to you all.

There really are not adequate words to speak of my dear friends and editors, Patricia and Donald Carnes. You guys with the rocket scientist minds (literally) and the Jesus-deep spirits that can see what the Lord is trying to say through me and translate it into words that people can even understand, I say simply, thank you. Thank you, thank you, thank you. You have taken this book which God wrote, and edited it as He would so that earthlings can know and better understand the heart of the Kingdom.

And to the Lord, my heart overflows as I ponder the miracle once again that You choose the weak and foolish things of the world as Your vessels to carry Your glory to a lost and dying world. Thank You, my Lord, for continuing to extend Your patience and grace to me, Your weak and flawed clay pot, in allowing me to work with You in the vineyards of the world. I love You, my King.

FOREWORD

The scene was intense. I was preaching powerfully in Indonesia concerning the new day we're entering. While speaking, a vision gradually came into focus before me. It was an unusual incident, one that I'd never before experienced while preaching. At first the vision seemed distant and blurry; like a visual anomaly. Perhaps I could rub my eyes and make it disappear. However the vision pressed its way closer until it loomed as a very clear large scene before me. It seemed to fill an entire wall. To say the least, it almost derailed my message that morning. I was so lost in it that I had to struggle to maintain my train of thought.

What was the vision? I saw this huge mountain emerging out of the sea. Just the tip was visible which loomed so far above the sea that snow capped its tip. At first I thought how strange! Then I realized that the vision I was seeing was linked to what I was preaching about, the new day. What I was "seeing" for the new day was this huge mountain that was just beginning to emerge from the sea.

God spoke in Daniel 2 that there is a kingdom which will become greater than every other kingdom; eventually it will crush every other kingdom. Daniel said to Nebudchadnezzar in Daniel 2:44-45,

> "And in the days of these kings the God of heaven will set up a kingdom which shall never be destroyed; and the kingdom shall not be left to other people; it shall break in pieces and consume all these kingdoms and it shall stand forever. Inasmuch as you saw that the stone was cut out of the mountain without hands, and that it broke in pieces the iron, the bronze, the clay, the silver, and the gold — the great God has made known to the king what will come to pass after this!"

Mountains scripturally represent kingdoms. The sea is often symbolic of people. Accordingly in this new day there is this Kingdom that is emerging out of a sea of people which will eventually overtake every other kingdom. It is the emergence of a people who understand that they the Church are a holy nation whose primary purpose is to preach, teach and release the Kingdom of God. This Kingdom paradigm is now emerging and will continue to grow until it overtakes our religious mindsets, transforming us into Kingdom minded believers.

When John the Baptist came preaching, he said, "Repent, for the Kingdom of Heaven is at hand." Jesus then repeated the same message, "repent, for the Kingdom of Heaven is at hand." His whole life purpose framing His activity on earth came from God. Through Jesus, God was restoring His purpose, to form a Kingdom that is above every other kingdom. Jesus, through His life, death and resurrection, apprehended the authority for people to become members of His Kingdom as well as to release and advance it. However this awareness has been lost through the neutralizing of Biblical truth. Deceptive changes transforming the Church from a powerful grass roots movement to an institutionalized organized religion dealt a blow to the Kingdom paradigm. But God!

What that vision I had was declaring was that we are in the midst of the re-emergence of the Church as the vehicle through which the Kingdom is released. The Church is not a building, it is you and I. Though we are in this earth, we are not of it. We are of another Kingdom, a holy nation. It is paramount that we now begin to comprehend what the Church, you and I, are all about. We are the releasers and advancers of the Kingdom of God.

It is to this challenge, that the Church step into its real identity, that Lora Allison has written this book. As I read this book, I became captured by her ability to artistically weave a tapestry of thoughts and truths concerning the Kingdom. She sets before us what we must understand in this hour, this new day.

As you read this book, keep in mind some principles of the Kingdom. Come to this book with a childlike spirit of wonderment, openness and excitement. Come to it with the simplicity of heart children have. Grasp the amazing mystery of the Kingdom as God opens your spirit to perceive beyond what your mind's eye can see. Children are not programmed to reject through analysis and skepticism that which is beyond them. When in a secure home, they simply trust their parents and therefore so easily follow and obey them. Recapture this childlike spirit as you read this book.

Jesus said, except you become as a little child, you can't enter the Kingdom of God. So let that childlike spirit overtake you and lead you through this book. It is a book of wonder, of revelation, of beauty, of truth; all expressing the truth of what this new day is all about. We are regaining the centrality of what the Church is about, the releasing and advancing of the Kingdom of God.

Lora Allison has written a masterful piece to help us regain our focus and to understand this day that we are entering, the days of the Kingdom of God.

Barbara J. Yoder
Senior Pastor and Lead Apostle
Shekinah Christian Church, Ann Arbor, MI, USA

Founder and Apostolic Leader
Breakthrough Apostolic Ministries Network

Chancellor, Breakthrough Leadership Institute
www.shekinahchurch.org
www.barbarayoderblog.com

INTRODUCTION

There's a fresh new wind picking up across the land. You know the kind, after a hot dry spell when suddenly you pick up the scent? Air begins to stir, the leaves rustle, and a new fragrance teases your nostrils. It's a quickening breeze, signaling coming rain. Now in the land of Christendom a faint and familiar message is beginning to waft across our senses. It's the message of the Kingdom. It's not new. It has been around since a man called John shouted in the wilderness: The Kingdom of Heaven is at hand!

The followers of Christ are a worn and ragged band of believers: weary, battle-scarred, skeptical; some indifferent, even bitter and disillusioned. Many with what could be called good reason. But take heart, a fresh move of the Spirit is on the way! An old new message is breaking in upon the consciousness of the most royal, destined Bride ever engaged. An old refrain with a new rhythm and a new sound is begging for attention. The Kingdom of Heaven is at hand!

We have heard about the Kingdom!

Yet have we really?

But it's been preached, taught, and proclaimed for over two thousand years.

Has it?

But many are living the New Testament church lifestyle and participating in a new apostolic reformation. That's all about the Kingdom.

One wonders?

Has there ever been clear understanding about the Kingdom of Heaven? Or has it been a mystery slowly unfolding on the consciousness of the Body of Christ since the beginning?

Now, as never before, there is a desperation driving many in this massive, world-wide Body of Christ. Without Truth we will perish.

But we know the Truth!

Do we?

But we preach the Truth!

Do we?

Perhaps mixture has slowly mudded the waters until Truth has been glazed over with ambition, pride and prejudice so that the perspectives generated by man's kingdoms, programs and agendas masquerade as Truth and actually breed deception.

Like a child so covered with mud that even he longs for clean pure water, the Body destined to be Christ's Bride is longing for purity and untainted Truth. Christendom is searching for fathers without personal agendas and leaders with a true desire to build up and strengthen God's children, just as Christ intended all along.

There is great need today to bring into clarity and focus what the Kingdom is and what God's heart and purposes are toward it. The gospel of the Kingdom is a simple message, but it is deeply profound at the same time. It is like elixir in the blood, like wind in the trees, and like leaven in the bread.

Ah, the Kingdom. Who can explain it? Jesus did, and everyone misunderstood and have continued to misunderstand, over the ages. But just as the Lord opened the eyes of the servant of Elijah, the Lord is opening our eyes, and bringing into focus great and wonderful things.

Comprehending these things of the Kingdom can be challenging when many have no idea Who the King really is. In order to align with His Kingdom, we must first KNOW Him, perceiving by His own love and wisdom this manifold and complex Light Being, before we can begin to align with His nature. The mystery of the Kingdom lies within the mystery of the King, and He desires that we seek Him out.

And even as we seek understanding of the nature of the King and His Kingdom, it is beneficial to perhaps redefine the progress of the manifestation of the Kingdom of God as it relates to the structure and relationships of the governing parts of the Body with the other functioning members and ministries. Proper structure or alignment can facilitate greater unity throughout the Body as well as with the Head, and thus cause the synergy of all to combust into greater fulfillment and manifestation of the Kingdom of God in earth as it is in Heaven.

There is a cry resounding from the throne room of the Most High, "Come up here and I will show you!" What a thrilling invitation! It is time to get out of the pit and out of prison. It is time to save the nation and to fulfill the destiny and dreams of long ago. It is time to reposition ourselves in alignment with the purposes and nature of the King and His Kingdom. This is the time for true alignment with His Body so that maximum purpose can be accomplished with maximum efficiency.

This is a signature moment. There is a colliding of kingdoms and wars and rumors of war on every hand. We are in a crucial and strategic valley of decision. This is the time for which we were born! This is an exciting time to be alive! This is the time for KINGDOM ALIGNMENT.

ONE

The Unfolding of the Kingdom of Heaven

The Kingdom of Heaven is an enigma that has perplexed, intrigued, and titillated the human brain perhaps more than any other riddle. There is a fascination in the subject of the Kingdom that compels us to think about it, read about it, pray about it, and to search for answers to our many questions. I have loved mysteries since my mother came into my room to catch me reading Nancy Drew books under the covers by flashlight late on a school night. The mystery of the Kingdom is infinitely more fascinating!

We find the phrase "mysteries of the Kingdom" first in Matthew 13:11. Like any true well-designed mystery, the more you pursue the Kingdom and the deeper you delve, more questions continue to be discovered than answers. A good plot is interwoven and deeply entwined like a priceless tapestry with great depth. The mystery of the Kingdom of Heaven is just so: deep, dark, and sweet.

The Bible says, "It is the glory of God to conceal a matter and the glory of kings to seek it out" (Proverbs 25:2). I have often wondered why the Lord seems to enjoy speaking to us in parables, dark sayings and enigmatic dreams. Thankfully one day there will be no need for these brain teasers or for prophecy (1 Corinthians 13:8), because all the smoke and mirrors will be gone and the Lamb Himself will be the only light we need. But until then, the scripture remains appropriate, "Behold, I will tell you a mystery..." (1 Corinthians 15:51). While revelation has been given, not everyone can perceive the truth of the mystery.

> He answered and said to them, "Because it has been given to you to know the mysteries of the kingdom of heaven, but to them it has not been given.
>
> For whoever has, to him more will be given, and he will have abundance; but whoever does not have, even what he has will be taken away from him.
>
> Therefore I speak to them in parables, because seeing they do not see, and hearing they do not hear, nor do they understand. And in them the prophecy of Isaiah is fulfilled, which says:
>
> 'Hearing you will hear and shall not understand,
> And seeing you will see and not perceive;
> For the hearts of this people have grown dull.
> Their ears are hard of hearing,
> And their eyes they have closed,
>
> Lest they should see with their eyes
> and hear with their ears,
> Lest they should understand with their hearts
> and turn, So that I should heal them.'
>
> But blessed are your eyes for they see, and your ears for they hear; for assuredly, I say to you that many prophets and righteous men desired to see what you see, and did not see it, and to hear what you hear, and did not hear it.
> Matthew 13:11-18, NKJV

The disciples wanted an earthly kingdom. So do I. And according to scripture, one day we will see it. But for now, we have a spiritual Kingdom that appears to be unfolding. How can it unfold, we wonder, when we know that God creates full grown. That which He makes, He makes complete. But did He create the Kingdom? Or does it exist as

He does, the alpha and the omega, beginning and end in itself, eternal and immortal?

Unfolding

Today in our world what has been created seems to still be evolving. Heaven is still invading earth. The people of God on earth are still instructed to pray, "Thy kingdom come...in earth as it is in heaven" (Matthew 6:10). So the Kingdom, while complete and fully operational in one realm, is still coming, unfolding or being gradually manifested in another.

When the disciples demanded what in the world Jesus was doing, the King of all the Universes replied, "My kingdom is not of this world" (John 18:36). And then they were taught the greatest mystery of all, "the Kingdom of God is within you" (Luke 17:21). Volumes can be written on just those two short phrases.

But after all that Jesus taught in such deep power and wisdom, and even after two thousand years of studying His Word, a large percentage of God's people—many of whom can quote reams of scripture and teach on many diverse Biblical subjects—still have either no knowledge of this mysterious Kingdom or certainly little understanding of it.

Which Kingdoms?

Human beings today continue to be very much captured by the world in which they live and operate, and most remain proponents of the axiom that man is the master of his own fate. And so, while professing Christ earnestly, mainstream Christians proceed on their own roadways arduously building what could be said to be their own "kingdoms."

For years we have all gotten away with it. The Body of Christ, often in the name of the "Kingdom," has steadily been burgeoning larger and more complicated. With so many churches, ministries, denominations and sects present worldwide, a questing pilgrim cannot easily recognize which is the true nature of Christ.

It is due to His matchless grace, endless mercy and unfailing love that we, in spite of ourselves and in the midst of all this confusion, are continuing to grow in the knowledge of God and preach the message of salvation. Yes, today as a Body at least each in his own fashion, we as His people still pursue Him, press on to know Him, and long and groan for His return.

But our world is rapidly changing. There is great acceleration on every hand. The phrases "Wars and rumors of wars" and "Why do the nations rage?" come to mind as world events seem to be careening out of control. Even those who have been touted and celebrated as leaders in Christendom are falling, and making unexpected and grievous turns in their very public lives. Many of even the least attuned to the voice of the Holy Spirit are hearing and recognizing an emphatic need for change and greater strength in order to survive an increasingly challenging universe.

The Call of the Kingdom

But into the melee of all this chaos as our spirits cry out to the Father for wisdom, comes an unexpected sound. It is the ringing call of the Kingdom, seeming to start from a distance, but drawing closer and closer. It is a thrilling sound. It is a sound few of us are able to understand. And it is a sound that every individual hears in their own unique way:

Prepare ye the way! Prepare the way of the Lord!
The Kingdom of Heaven is at hand!

There are those today who are not so busy that they do not hear. Comprehending what they are hearing is another issue. Many are at least attempting to obey a call for change. Like a chapter eleven bailout when a business fails, there is now a necessary *Reorganization* happening in the Body of Christ. In order to continue successfully, there must be structural change. The shaking has been and will continue to be tremendous. As we hold on and seek wisdom, we realize that this change which is part of God's destiny for all of us, has become imminent, crucial and necessary.

The King is stepping up the program. The cloud is moving. The building of the Kingdom is going to another level. The Lord is taking all of His lively stones, and while placements are changing, the superstructure is going up, and up, and UP. We struggle and pant to keep up with Him. We strive to recognize road signs and to find our way in an increasingly unfamiliar landscape. Really we could be exasperated. Just when we think we have reached something we know, it changes AGAIN. The rules and boundaries seem to continue to change.

And the Lord says, Of course they are changing. You are growing, and to continue to grow, you must change. In My mercy, I am changing the playing field. I am changing the players. I, the Master Architect, Chief Cornerstone, and the Builder, have brought in the next set of blueprints, and together we are going forward.

PERCEPTION OF THE KINGDOM

So shall He startle and sprinkle many nations, and kings shall shut their mouths because of Him; for that which has not been told them shall they see, and that which they have not heard shall they consider and understand.

Isaiah 52:15, AMP

Understanding beckons and glimmers in the distance: something to be reached. Like a gleaming citadel, a destination all of itself. Always it was just out of reach, just beyond ourselves, and we longed for even the semblance of knowing. Being in unfamiliar territory, we look around, and like Lots's wife, find ourselves turning to look behind. But in so doing we turn our backs on that very thing so desired. If we concentrate and attempt to focus, the distance grows greater, but if we wait, the image sharpens while remaining outside of our understanding. Yet that's the very ideal and the thing so sought after: understanding that is beyond our own.

understanding beyond our own

The Kingdom is like that. We've always known it was there, but it was too far, too blurry, and seemed just beyond our reach and ahead of our present progress. The parables and shadows we read only thicken the atmosphere and make comprehension almost undesirable since we seek it but never quite reach our goal. Then the question arises: have we been there all of this time and have just now recognized it? Are we living in the midst of our destination and have not the wit to recognize and verbalize the landscape?

The Kingdom is our destination. It is our home. Our place of residency. Our destiny. Our hope. Our fulfillment. Our ideal. It is the air that keeps us alive, and the drink that aerates our bodies and makes life to bloom in spite of ourselves. The Kingdom, like leaven, causes everything to grow and expand and thrive. But it is not heavy and hard to digest. It is light and expanding. Acknowledging residency in the Kingdom is like watching the air filling a huge balloon that we know is about to bear us aloft into the heavens. It is unsubstantial yet it is that which will hold our weight and even those around us as we leave terra firma and lift off.

The Kingdom of Heaven lifts us up from the heaviness of plodding firmly on the familiar ground, earth bound and miserable. Living there is like a breath of relief even while the fear of falling fills our senses. The only thing more frightening is that we are not alone. And all around us are many who are in the same free fall, with the same sense of reaching their destination and yet not understanding where, what, when and how. All of our familiar pertinent information now no longer applies. The language is different, the sounds are different, and the air is rarified. Sight, well, what meets our eyes is so new that even sound is preferable, so scary does it seem when we open our eyes.

What we have longed for is upon us. Will we have the courage to embrace it? Will we have the hope to sustain ourselves and discipline ourselves to grasp it? Or will we, like the reluctant wife, turn our gaze back, and in losing our balance, freeze forever in the past while the delightful future streams onward like the airless wind?

what we have longed for is upon us

Leading Amidst Winds of Change

Leaders cannot grab a toehold. Followers manage better, but they cannot lead others because they are not called to be leaders. Leaders cannot lead because they are still attempting to lead as they did in the past, but it no longer works. Frustrated, they give up while just on the brink of leading the most significant advent of destiny the world has ever known.

Their weaknesses loom like huge manholes just waiting to trip them up in a timeless forever prison of their own making. Many don't survive. Many wish they would not. Many in the midst of unknowable reality so long for the familiar that they give up on the future, even while still praying that it will come to pass. May it never be!

God grant leaders not only the grace and strength to embrace the new, but the ability to lose the ever present crucible of the need to understand. For the process of understanding was always a haze, a shade, a fog, and a nameless wondering not even close to the rock solid reality of knowing that we thought it was. Even comprehension is not as we thought it was. Comprehension now has new dimensions and boundaries in this new reality beyond our understanding. We liked the notion of love beyond our boundaries. We liked the thought of peace that passes understanding. We were intrigued by the knowledge that God is beyond our comprehension.

But beyond these familiar concepts, when reality in our perception comes face to face with the possible manifestation of the beyond-our-understanding, we are frightened away from the confrontation like a deer running in the darkness and suddenly blinded by great and brilliant light. Caught, we come to an abrupt halt in our headlong flight. Frozen, we don't know what to do. And this, the crux of the matter, frightens us beyond belief. We don't know what to do, nor how to be responsible for great numbers of people who know even less than we do. It is the ultimate nightmare. The blind leading the blind.

The coming of Kingdom perspectives can seem like that. Blind to the new, and leading a mass behind us who only see as far as we do ourselves, the whole procession is suspended between two realities. The kingdoms of this earth, and the Kingdom of our God. Caught between two worlds, yet leading, guiding, administrating, and God forbid, teaching as we go. No one wants to *caught between two worlds* admit it, indeed, how can we, if we want them to continue to follow. And follow they must, or we are all lost. *Lost?* But we know where we are going, that's why they follow us. *Really?*

The secret must never be told. The leaders don't know where we are going. Or at least they only know what they themselves drew as the yearly map. And they know each turn, and each budget according to that map and those turns. So when the Kingdom of Heaven interferes, what then? Who loses? The leaders or the followers?

Both lose, if we keep OUR blueprints and if we keep OUR maps and if we continue to make OUR turns. So we are at an impasse, headed by leaders who can't lead because they don't know where they are going when the new orders come in. And in their inability to follow the sealed, unfamiliar and incomprehensible orders, they continue to lead, willfully, in the wrong direction and in the wrong process, to the wrong destination.

Carried by the Lord

Comprehension of the Kingdom beckons in the distance like a mirage. The edges sharpen in and out again and we wonder, is it real? If we go there will it solidify into something practical and useable and livable? And so, in failing to understand, we must fall, once again, into the everlasting arms. And leaning on Him, we are carried from that familiar, often cruel but comfortable reality, to new dimensions, new heights and new, higher ground.

fall into the everlasting arms

Carry us, Lord. Carry us beyond ourselves. Beyond our present understanding. Beyond our present reality. Beyond our present prisons of thought and the confines of our present reality. Carry us Lord, on the wings of your Word. Let us respond to the voice saying, "Come up here and I will show you…" And we looked and we saw, and we heard the voice, and suddenly we were in the Spirit (Revelation 4:1).

Just as the ground falls away and our plane lifts, carrying our control and our lives with it, so the Body of Christ is lifting off, and our control and our lives with it. Give us the courage to go with the Lamb, whithersoever He goes. For He is giving us the keys to the Kingdom, our destin-y-ation.

> And He replied to them, "To you it has been given to know the secrets and mysteries of the kingdom of heaven, but to them it has not been given."
> Matthew 13:11, AMP

THE UNFOLDING OF THE KINGDOM

And so, the Kingdom is unfolding all around us, even as we look and do not see. Like the butterfly in the chrysalis, the Kingdom has come and has been expanding and unfolding without our knowledge or even our understanding. It does not need our permission, or our endorsement. What we believe or even preach has no real effect on its development. It is not our Kingdom. It is, yet it is not. It is a supernatural entity, an immortal realm that God has ordained without our approval. We were told of its coming and taught of its power, even while we longed for a physical king and the comfort of physical rule.

And so, after a time, human beings decided to take a hand in its making, to speed along the process so to speak. That which is supernatural and invisible and immortal began to be governed by that which is not. Seemingly, God has allowed this state of affairs, but what is His heart concerning it? Like an avalanche moving down a hill, the process has gained momentum as teaching, perspectives and church entities vie with one another for first place, top visibility, and the most followers.

Heavenly Activity

But there is a quickening in the Spirit. There is a shoring up of angelic activity, and there is a stirring in heavenly realms. Something is up. Something is about to happen. Changes are being made. Human guards are changing, and exposure is bringing a great shaking in what the world's Christians often have called the Kingdom. Can it be that what has commonly been known as the Kingdom is really a false and flimsy façade made by human hands, while the house made by God is slowly unfolding and materializing before our eyes that are just now beginning to see?

There is a great anticipation in the invisible realms. The Word is creating again. In fact, it has never stopped. But the eyes of the Body of Christ are opening and revelation of the inner workings of Christendom are being made apparent. There are dirty seams underneath, but steel girders as well. The unchangeable God is allowing comprehension to strike the Body of Christ as they see things they never wished to see, alongside many things they have yearned to see all along.

In one sense, the Kingdom is not actually unfolding, but it is our perception of it that is widening, broadening, and becoming quickened by the Holy Spirit. The Spirit of revelation is guiding us into the Truth of what we are about, and correcting our aim and focus even at the speed with which we are moving. There is an acceleration as we shoot through the realms of time and space, and we begin to realize that God is not bound into those realms, and thus is not frightened by this speed in the way that we seem to be.

Church is changing, and people are increasingly disappointed by and restless with church as we know it. Buildings are closing and pastors are leaving the ministry. Sin is being exposed, and many of the most vocal against it are secretly carrying out their own version, in the underseams of what is known. Meanwhile, the true Kingdom is pulling, drawing, and insisting, much like a huge magnet that is invisibly throwing all of our metallic set-in-place structures way out of kilter.

The true Kingdom is taking over, because it must. By its very nature, it must. That which can be shaken is disintegrating, leaving the incomprehensible, monolithic, vast, and majestic mystery of the ages, standing as it has always stood. Those who are bound to the earth's version of the Kingdom are going down with that which they have created. But that which GOD has created has and will stand forever. We are choosing today on which line we stand.

As the Kingdom "unfolds," we as Kingdom residents are growing, shifting and changing from glory to glory and from revelation to revelation. If we don't change we don't grow. The Kingdom is unfolding within us and we are stretching inside ourselves to accommodate drastic change. Our minds must be renewed to keep up with it, lest it unfold within and we are unable to recognize what is so near to us.

KINGDOM DOMINION

The very word kingdom refers to the rule, domain, or dominion of a king. The ruler reigns over, supersedes, even controls in a sense, his domain. He sets the boundaries and the laws; he governs according to his "world viewpoint" and perspectives.

In today's world of independent thinking, we don't like the word control. It suggests all manner of undesirable and perhaps even unhealthy situations. We want to be the master of our own fate, so to speak, and we want total authority over all that touches our own lives, work, and sphere of influence. Entering into and participating, then, in an invisible kingdom with an invisible king is definitely a challenge. It is impossible for many, unless they undergo strong changes of ideas and perspectives.

Jesus and the centurion gave us a glimpse of Kingdom authority in a life and death situation (Matthew 8:8-9). This soldier of authority in his own world recognized the authority of a realm beyond his understanding and bowed before it. His humility and obedience brought deliverance and healing to his servant. The dominion of the King and the principles of Kingdom rule were actively employed and a miracle was the result.

The throne of God stands upon His authority, and this authority extends to every corner and space of His realm, His dominion absolute. What is often not readily apparent to the casual onlooker is the goodness, kindness, generosity, and love which are so tightly interwoven into the nature of this dominion and authority as to be indivisible. The quality and nature of THIS rule and dominion is determined solely and completely by the character of this intense Being of unimaginable power who, oddly enough to some, is also known as "Abba, Father."

Accepting this dominion rule of power is an initial component in becoming Kingdom residents. But perhaps knowing the King, a concept virtually unknown in earth's kingdoms, is the key to our willing acceptance and thus obedience in this immortal, indivisible Kingdom.

knowing the King

Just as many in their own various countries are unaware of much of the inner workings of human government but governed by it just the same, so it is with the Kingdom. Change and growth in ourselves comes gradually alongside recognition and understanding of Kingdom dominion, even while we live with Him and enjoy His benefits.

While the Kingdom of Heaven will cause unheralded change in the organized church, the greatest changes of all will come within living beings, or lively stones, if you will. Because that is where the Kingdom resides— within the cracked, marred and frail vessels of human earth. That's it: God's light in the clay pots of Gideon's meager army, about to overcome the greatest foe they could imagine (Judges 7:19-20).

How far are we willing to go? How far does He want to take us? Do we really want self-imposed boundaries on the destiny our Creator has planned for us? So again we ask, how far are we willing to go? We have not evidenced, in general, much capacity for crucifixion. Can we remain who we think we are, desire to be, and intend to be, while changing rapidly and with necessity into what we must be, all at the same time?

> And saying, "Repent (think differently; change your mind, regretting your sins and changing your conduct), for the kingdom of heaven is at hand."
>
> Matthew 3:2, AMP

WINDOW OF HOPE

Through the window a new dawn lights the horizon. A new day is on the threshold. And seers peering into the realm of God's mighty Spirit see a vast Light rising in the darkness of this present age. Prophets everywhere are calling mankind to the window to see history in the making. And man, on his way to the window, wonders if his ship is finally coming in. Just like the disciples who looked for an earthly kingdom and a reigning king, man is looking for some kind of "reward" for his labors. He is immediately relating coming change to, "How will this benefit me personally?"

There are many types of payment, many types of reward and many types of currency. Man is always looking for his reward and his payment, constantly demanding to know what the currency is, or the medium of exchange. If I do this, what will I get, and if I do that what will be given to me? Man is always looking for a return on the act of his will and on the result of his labors. He doesn't want to work for nothing. He doesn't want to put forth any effort without the comfort of knowing that immediately something will come back. So he works with his eye on the payment; he labors with his attention on the reward.

He is trapped in the film of a time/space dimension, always looking from one frame to the next frame, in order to have the courage to proceed from one place into the next. But God is taking the foot of man and causing it to step upon the waters of eternity: *step out upon the waters of eternity* out of one realm into another.

And the payment of his labors in this time/space dimension as his eye is on the road ahead is a payment in hope. For his reward of hope opens his eyes at last to see his release from this prison of time, and from this bondage of doing in order to get, and walking ahead in exchange for something. The payment for obedience to the King of Kings is the hope of a better realm. It is the hope of a better life, the hope of a greater understanding, the hope of a broader expectation, the hope of a deeper encouragement, the hope of a keener joy, the hope of expansive revelation, and the hope of eternal existence.

Hope is a window through which man can see God's plan. It is like the window on a spaceship. Inside the spaceship, except for weightlessness, the spaceman is surrounded by the things of his own world. But through the window of the spaceship lies an expanse of uncharted territory, foreign experience, and different air. The spaceman is well content to stay within the confines of his own understanding, with his instruments, his calculations, his measurements and his spacesuit.

But the Lord desires that man would leap through the window of hope into that other place where he is not bound by the cords of the adversities of life nor chained to the doors of anxiety. He is not lashed to the post of diligence; the manacles upon his ankles don't hobble him to the walls of anger. The hymns, songs and praises of deliverance have set the captives free, that man may fly from the evidences of his terror out of the dungeons of despair through the window of hope, leaving behind familiar instruments of bondage.

So many choose to remain shackled by familiarity. So many would rather submit to the tortures of the known than to leap out through the door of hope into the unknown joys and delights of another realm, another time, another space, another experience: prisoners of hope. No longer prisoners of desire in a realm of legalism and knowledge, but prisoners of hope, having left the old behind, content to walk according to the life of the Spirit. The dawn or the breaking

shackled by familiarity

of the day is the promise, the hope, of the fullness of the day. The dawning of a new day is upon the horizon.

> Because of the tender mercy of our God, with which the Sunrise from on high shall visit us, to shine upon those who sit in darkness and the shadow of death, to guide our feet into the way of peace.
>
> Luke 1:78-79, NASU

Man will walk by the light of the sun and no longer strive in the dimness and shadows of the moon. For though the moon was a blessing in the darkness, in the light of the sun there will be no need for the moon, one having moved from the lesser light to the greater light. Then one has moved from the work/reward system through the door of hope into the cycles of life and become whirlwinds and fireballs of the energy of God, rolling through eternity.

Now man roars through uncharted space with no thought of

mileage or effort or labor or payment or reward. But he is content in the privilege of going, content to generate, to operate, content to burst forth with life, content to explode with the regenerative miraculous and joyous nature of Him Who is the wind and the rain and the thunder and the song. In that day, man has moved into the realm where there is no darkness, and where he has become one with the vast ball of Fire around which the universe lives and moves and has its being.

This is a journey which is required if we are to move with our whole heart, like Abraham of old, into the unknown realms of God, holding on to Him with all our might. The Kingdom is calling us in this hour. What will we respond?

Do we truly care about this Kingdom? Do we evidence hunger to know and explore God's purposes and realms? If the Kingdom of Heaven is our God's sphere of authority, dominion, and power; how can we not make all possible efforts to comprehend this mystery, and to align ourselves with its principles? Do we have the courage to boldly go where we have never gone before?

The Kingdom of Heaven is at hand! Our answer must be yes! Whatever we must do to align ourselves with God's realms, let us do it with all alacrity! We must leap through the window of hope and hasten to do His will! To His slightest desire, to His quietest whisper, let us respond with resounding acquiescence.

Let our focus and our greatest passion be to know and please our King. Let us grow, change, and expand into the designs of the Most High. Let us not be found hiding and uncertain. Let us run this race with all diligence toward the mark of the high call in Christ Jesus. And let us align ourselves with Him and with one another in the Kingdom of Heaven!

Two

Kingdom Perspectives

I grew up in a small, country town in Louisiana, "in the middle of nowhere" as the saying goes. As a young Baptist girl, I was practically raised on the front pew of our tiny church where I experienced the Word of God from a very early age. I can remember Christmas Eve nights alone in my bedroom with an old, simple radio. I would tune in from station to station and pause each time I heard Handel's *Messiah* being sung. I spent hours wading through distant stations and radio noise, looking for it year after year. And I was thrilled each time I stumbled upon it, a distant sound of splendorous life from another world.

I had never been present at a concert of that piece, nor even present at any large chorus or orchestra. So the majestic music resounded through my being, touching chords deep within myself that I didn't understand. The pull and magic of each stolen moment with the ancient words and inspired music seemed to call out to me from another land, from a shining citadel beckoning and reaching out to me.

Now, so many years later, I know that that wonderful call came from the life of the Kingdom. Now I can recognize that the anointing and life of heavenly realms was my destiny then, as it is now. I have come to understand that that life is Christ, Jesus the anointed one, the one true God and the King and ruler of a mysterious place called the Kingdom of God.

The recognition of distant realms beyond our experience is not new to most, but many dismiss it as pipe dreams, imagination, or wishful thinking. Unfortunately, most leave the unfamiliar feelings without exploring the Word of God and connecting the faint tremors of experience with it. But the Lord is putting all things together, and connecting them for us in this very hour. The shining destination ahead of us is hardly a dream, or an unfounded wish. In this day the current move of the Holy Spirit is guiding us into greater understanding of the truth of the Kingdom of God, and into the knowledge of the Life of the Kingdom.

THE LIFE OF THE KINGDOM

And the LIFE of the Kingdom! It is an effervescent, ebullient, buoyant life, bursting with exuberant joy, hope, and energy! How can one truly describe this life for which everyone seeks and from which so many turn away, both at the same time. How difficult it is to grasp that the very essence of what is longed for could be so thoroughly rejected and disdained in the same heart!

effervescent, ebullient, buoyant life

In the parables, Jesus often spoke of the creative, multiplying nature of the Kingdom. He spoke of the principles of this new life, even as He preached to residents of death. He spoke to the blind and the lepers and the lame. Is it any different today? Whether blind in spirit or leprous in nature, all today need the life that He offers freely, without price.

As He watched the multitudes run to Him, He also watched the crowds turn away. How interesting to wonder who will choose life, and who will choose death. He sat on the mountainsides and His voice reached them all, in all stages and levels of prominence in their world. What was it inside of them that turned their lives down each road?

What is it inside of us that causes us to make the choices that we make? Our decisions which affect so many are often made with such little discrimination. And yet before us lies the ultimate, destined, pinnacle of human existence, free for our choosing.

As we contemplate Kingdom life, let us consider Jesus, the out-raying of the divine, the exact representation of the Father, the pearl of great price and the lily of the valley. Exactly what is it about Him that would cause one to turn away from Him? Obviously, it could not be HIM. It must be about us. And isn't that always the case? It is always about ME, the mighty I. How would this King affect my life, ambitions, and goals? What "freedoms" would I lose?

I can remember just those kinds of thoughts in my pre-Kingdom days. I was afraid that I would lose control of my future if every decision I made was essentially made by someone else. It wasn't until much later in my life, after fires and floods and tragedy and trauma, that the idea of someone else began to be comforting. To have someone else who can tell me what to do, which road to travel and which pitfall to avoid. How many years of life must it take for us to gratefully accept our place in this matchless unidentifiable structure so substantial and yet often so indiscernible?

A large part of our dilemma, of course, is that we are making spiritual decisions with our unregenerated, carnal, and natural mind, which does not, neither can it, discern spiritual things. This too is an impasse. At some point in each of our lives, our spirit must rise up to overtake the understanding, and we must make that walk-out-on-the-water choice. Happily, we are usually unaware that this is just the first of all the thousands of decisions to come just like it, as a normal part of Kingdom life.

Gradually, we lose fear and dread when we must rely on God totally, and resurrection life begins to seep into our blood and our veins. The DNA of our heavenly Father begins to run like sweet elixir in our being. Momentum builds, and exciting truth breaks in upon our previously darkened consciousness. LIFE! This is true LIFE! And just as one newly in love, colors seem brighter, and birds sing more sweetly. The wind blows so gently, and all of creation sings of the One whom we love. And so it remains, until the cares of the world begin to drag us down, down, down, all the way to the place where we were before, or even lower yet.

So how does one maintain this wonderful life? How do we LIVE in the Kingdom, breathe its air, sing its songs, and run with its wind, while walking on this earth? Is this a possibility, or are we only enduring here until we are there, leaving this earth and all we love. How indeed, do we LIVE KINGDOM LIFE?

Transformation of our Natural Mind

First and foremost, we must continue to be transformed with the renewing of our minds. We must learn to think as He thinks and respond as our renewed minds indicate. But changing our thought processes is a lifetime pursuit, we sometimes think with despair!

> ...because the mind of the flesh [with its carnal thoughts and purposes] is **hostile** to God, for it does not submit itself to God's Law; indeed it cannot.
>
> Romans 8:7, AMP

Sometimes it seems that working with my rebellious body and all of its various complaints is infinitely preferable to working with my thinking, thinking, always thinking brain. Teaching that runaway train to brake and take heed is such a daunting challenge. So much has been taught and written on this subject, and yet we continue to fight what often seems to be a losing battle.

The following is a prophetic passage that the Lord once gave me concerning the nature of the carnal mind.

> "For my mind, yes, the carnal mind is jaded and weary, always looking for something new, never satisfied, restless, irritable and bored. It is imperious, dictatorial, and insistent upon its own way. My mind definitely has a personality of its own, a very dominant personality. It wishes exaltation and proper respect. It demands fealty and supremacy. It is a snobbish organ, disdainful and proud. It is also very insecure, and sensitive about its inabilities.
>
> My mind is intrusive, an intruder, in fact. It doesn't like the spirit, because it senses that the spirit will rule one day. And it is like a deposed king, very, very hateful, and frantic. It is grasping. But the light is coming, and those who have walked in darkness will see a great light. And instead of annihilation, my mind will find that refreshing is on the way. My mind will find new ways to learn. My

mind will no longer rule, it's true. But in dying, it will find new life. It will find real peace, because my mind will stay upon the One who created it.

It will have the attributes of a Mind greater than man could ever conceive. A mind that reaches past all time, all space and all dimension. A mind that does all and far more than it always wanted to in the past. It will break the time barrier, the sound barrier, and all other barriers. It will run free and weightless and clean. It will zoom and swoop and circle and dive. It will lark and dance and joy. The regions of my mind that were once a desert will become a garden. A watered garden. A garden spot.

There will be wonder and joy—the joy of discovery. For now there is no reason to be jaded and bored and depressed and sad. For Oh, you new mind, you will never come to the end of your God. For there will be knowledge upon knowledge upon knowledge, and world upon world. Exploring, running fast upon the waters and riding high upon the winds. O, you mighty mind of man, you must rise out of the old places. Out of the old trenches, you must dust off your wings and you must leave the old waste places, the places of darkness. For the lamps are being lit and the fires kindled for the greatest of all adventures: the journey into LIGHT." [1]

The Awakening of Light

Once I picked up a book by a famous prophet and had a most interesting reaction. It felt like living, tangible light in my hands. This is Kingdom life! This is the thread that must be allowed to run through all of our daily, hour by hour living.

The mind is energized and transformed by light. The rarefied emotions race and rest, fueled, directed and fired by the energy and power of the life and light that is Christ, holding all things together. To

---

[1]   Paragraphs from the author's work, *Overcomer: The Emerging Church of the Third Day*

be freed from the machinations and unreliable predictions of our carnal minds! Wouldn't we rather be racing with the wind of the Spirit and smelling the fragrant incense of His presence; than struggling with the bondages and required crutches of walking in the world's kingdoms?

In this present hour the Lord of the Harvest is sending out a compelling call:

Kingdom life! Kingdom life!
Leave the old ways behind and be renewed into the glory of
Kingdom life! The stresses and strains of the darkness of this present age are not burdens which you must of necessity bear.

You are not of this world. Why then will you continue to bear its burdens and be ruled by its aggravations, irritations, fears, and torments?

Come and drink the water of life without price!

Come! Come up higher where the air is pure, sharp and pungent with the newness, with the effervescent newness of life!

My life renews, refreshes, restores and pardons.
Forgiveness is part of this air, and so is freedom.

I will free you from your diseases and addictions.

I will become your only need.

Come! In this hour, Come!

It seems odd to realize that this call is not just for the heathen kingdoms of the world, for the ultimate sinner, or for the one so lost in the wilderness of daily pleasures. This call is also to those who have "known" the Lord, some for many years. This call is for pastors, ministers, evangelists and missionaries across this broad expanse called earth.

This call is for those who have always been sure that they see, yet are as unaware of the life of the Kingdom as many who have never heard the phrase. As the call goes out, it carries with it a wake-up anointing. It carries that thrilling, life-restoring rise up and walk anointing that will open eyes which have been *wake-up* asleep to the fullness of God, even while working *anointing* and laboring on His behalf.

Therefore He says, Awake, O sleeper, and arise from

the dead, and Christ shall shine (make day dawn) upon
you and give you light.

Ephesians 5:14, AMP

Come to the waters and drink!
You who are thirsty, come!

So many laboring in the fields of the Lord are thirsty for the
sweetness of His presence. They are hungering after the essence of the
King. The spirit within them is now urgently pressing them onward,
past the daily work that once so satisfied them, and past the titles
and acknowledgements that brought such satisfaction and seeming
fulfillment. This season is not satisfied with old victories and past glory.
This season presses and rings with the call, a new call, an urgent and
insistent call,

Come up higher!
There is more than you know!
It's the life of the Kingdom!
It's the health and wealth of the unknown!

Revelation is bursting upon the scenes of earthly life like the great
burst of the sun in all of its splendor after the dark night of the soul. No
matter who you are or where you have been, listen and respond to the
call. There is more than you know! The active, sharp and powerful life
of the Kingdom is reaching out; it is moving out to draw us to run after
the King. It is enveloping and unfolding to bring us to repentance and
conviction and a hunger beyond any we have ever known.

For this Kingdom is bringing forth sons, the ones long awaited.
They are waking from sleep; they are coming forth from the graves
of despair and earthly sorrows. They are springing up in newness of
life with fresh steps and fresh vigor to proclaim the good news of the
Kingdom.

The awakening in progress will bring focus and great change of
direction. The blinders are coming off and the bridles and traces are
falling away as the great steeds of the Lord freshen and scent the distant
roar of the coming battle. The mighty war horses trained for battle and
kept in holding fields until this moment are rising up across the earth.
There is no moratorium on age, physical condition, or on past history.

There is no requirement that they cannot pass. For wrapped into the call is the ability to run the race. Wrapped into the ringing tones of the voice of the Master is the energizing ability to meet the challenge. We were born for this! They recognize the time, they know the voice. The vestiges of sleep fall away. The lethargy and malaise of the past seasons are gone in a moment. The life of the Kingdom has moved on them and they thrill to answer the call.

New mantles are falling and old mantles are passing away. Old guards and sentinels so faithful in past seasons are hearing the call and moving rapidly and suddenly to new posts and new challenges. What seems like upheaval is simply what we would know as the changing of the guard. The watchman is sounding the alarm, and the resultant change is like the wind blowing across fields of grain. It blows, moving all alive, then recedes, leaving its mark in the wake.

In the heavens, the hosts of the Lord of Sabbaoth are watching, waiting, and running with their missions. Activity is everywhere. Something is afoot! New orders are going out! All the hosts of the Lord are on alert, as the Spirit moves and directs and energizes and causes to live again. The thrilling activity, the pulsing power, the LIFE OF THE KINGDOM is moving along.

The divine purpose and call is standing tall in all the regions of heaven and earth, and the honor and glory of the King's edict is being carried out. He has spoken! The thunder shakes and rings across creation! Lightning flashes and His arrows go forth! The King rides again and the hosts move into place. This season is beyond our understanding. The Lord of the battle is riding victoriously, taking us with Him. We answer and follow, just as we were born to do. This is our life. This is the life of the Kingdom.

The King rides again

KINGDOM LANGUAGE

There are exciting ways and varied opportunities to avail ourselves of Kingdom life. Here we can find many arenas and avenues of escape from the plodding existence so abhorrent in the world. To appropriate the Kingdom is to leave the ways of the earth far, far behind and to learn another set of senses and perceptions. What is so readily apparent and repugnant in the world can disappear in the blink of an eye, but of course then we question our sanity. Anything familiar suddenly becomes more comfortable than the new untried terrain before us.

How shall we comport ourselves? How will we act, think, and most importantly, reason in this new world? Ah, there is the crux of the matter. Reason. Though the Lord God, the Father said, "Come now, and let us reason together," instinctively we know that in this brave new world, this reason has very little to do with the way we currently think (Isaiah 1:18). Otherwise why would we be so uncomfortable? Generally we are extremely comfortable with our thoughts. We love our thoughts. We love the way our mind works, and we take great pride in what we acknowledge to be our "reason." So when God initiates "reason together," immediately we are restless, cautious, and even fearful. Why would this be so?

Because the Kingdom seems to have a different language. A language that, instead of simply expressing what we want it to express, is often a combatant, a deterrent, or a challenge to everything we know, want to know, or, more importantly, want to do. This new articulation, so foreign to human desire, drives us in directions we do not want to go. It challenges, even threatens our preferred way of life. It often shouts down our smug, prideful intellectual comprehension with a quiet, almost unintelligible murmur, so soft and innocuous and gentle that it is extremely frightening in its non-threatening yet firm way. It is pertinent to recognize that the language of the Kingdom is, after all, the language of God.

Learning to Listen

In ourselves we have longed to hear the voice of God. We have prayed and wept bitter tears in search of communication from our King, our Lover, our Bridegroom, our Father, our Comforter, our Brother, our Solace, our Help in ages past, and our Guide. And in those rare moments when the Voice comes, golden in its sweetness and its mellifluous and harmonious sounds, our life willingly disappears before the sheer majesty of the fact that He Spoke.

Why then, when the language of the Kingdom comes in other ways, at other times, with other purposes, are we so resistant? Surely we should desire to know our King in all of His aspects and ways?

Surely we desire His counsel and direction as only the great Creator can give?

Perhaps we only recognize the beauty of His voice when His Presence accompanies it and we receive its comfort because we desire that particular direction; and also because nothing seems to be required of us at that moment? Yet when in other arenas not directly involving His majestic Presence we are required to go into the vineyards and the sheepfolds, what then? What happens when the language of the Kingdom becomes directly involved with the OTHER aspects of daily involvement in Kingdom life? Namely the WORK, and the contact with perhaps less savory elements? Suddenly the language of the Kingdom becomes less desirable, less thrilling, and much more challenging to our preferred modes of operation.

Could it be that we Kingdom dwellers have selective and highly refined hearing that effectively and automatically blocks out all lines of communication but that one, golden, splendid rare moment with HIM? So how many times and situations and open doors and admonitions have we missed over the years, and how many chances to grow and give and serve have we missed in disobedience? The thought of it should strike terror to our hearts.

Could it have been HIS voice that we were ignoring? Could it be that we who have been saved and filled with His Spirit and serving Him all of our lives have not effectively learned to recognize and use the language of the Kingdom? Could we have missed our way in not one but many areas because we have only been open to certain nuances of His voice but not others? Have we been ignoring the King?

In the kingdoms of this earth that would be a capital offense. Ignoring the voice, the language, and the directions of earthly rule would result in imprisonment, or in many other forms of creative punishment. Oh! Would it be the king himself who is doing the punishing? Not really? Not personally? Therefore, it must be the structure that he has set into place. So in effect, as residents of a country, choosing not to listen or to obey the rules would be a sort of self-choice punishment? Oh. This is a novel way to look at it. So it's not really personal, in a sense. We refuse to listen to the language. Then as a result we don't obey the ways of life set up for the common good of the people, and we reap the punishment set up for those situations? Exactly!

Rest in the Change

So in the Kingdom of Heaven, there is structure, language, and way of life. Willfully keeping our own independence from that divine system will have grave consequences, affecting first and foremost our own quality of life. But depending upon who is following us, it can also affect large numbers of people and systems and habitations and regions.

There is coming an overhaul, a shoring up, a redefining, and a clearing out of the world's ways and systems that have been brought into the Kingdom. No longer seeming to "fit in," there will be an exposing first, then a purging of the Kingdom as we know it. And then, the Kingdom may be manifested as HE knows it. And all of creation, which has been groaning for this very manifestation, can begin to experience peace.

Rest is coming to the chaos that creation became so many eons ago, and manifestation of divine will and purpose is growing readily more apparent. It will come in the language of the Kingdom. It will come in the ways of the Kingdom. It will not be

rest is coming to chaos

dealt with in the world's ways, but in the ways of the Most High, the Sovereign God, whose ways and thoughts are not those of the world.

That is the reason there has been so much confusion in the minds and hearts of even the seasoned saints and residents of the Kingdom. There has been mixture, kingdom superimposed upon Kingdom. Discerning the layers, and dividing and accurately handling the word of Truth in the midst of it has been the challenge. But we will all be changed. Thank God! The structures and monuments to intellect will come down, and humility will precede true knowledge, as revelation sweeps through the eternal Kingdom of the ages.

Patience will be required in the process of such great change. Long suffering, kindness, and acceptance will be vital. Long held dreams will appear like mirages slowly gaining substance, but not without a price. Listen! Listen for the language, the voice, and the nuances of the communication from the Most High. Be willing to hear, no matter the cost or the requirement. The requirement could mean everything, all we have known, all we have desired, or hoped to be. But then HIS will and purpose, being so much higher and deeper than ours, will overtake the old longings. Then we will wonder how we ever thought that it could be important anyway, in the face of such Divine Majesty and the establishment of things literally beyond our comprehension or imagining.

His dreams or ours. Could there be a choice? Oh yes, there always has been and always will be. But the difference in this new season is that we will, by choice, now have greater understanding of the difference in these dreams. We will see, finally, how mean and small and HUMAN our dreams were, and how vast and far reaching and immortal, His. You know, many times our dreams were born by Him, but we quickly took them over, and eventually they became ours, hardly resembling His original idea at all. There will be a rebirth of these dreams, and they will be restored to their former splendor, shining with the glory of the eternal, and dripping with the anointing that breaks the yokes of the kingdoms of the world simply by being— simply by their very existence.

rebirth of
dreams

How the redemptive, restorative God forgives, and heals, and causes us to live again! Listen for His voice, His language, His slightest murmuring in the night. No matter what He says, no matter what it might mean. Try not to process it with your former way of thinking, before it hardly gets out of His mouth. Pray that He give you the wisdom to let it lie, growing and gestating in your heart, while the mighty Holy Spirit hovers over it. He will watch it lie, deep within your being until it has settled into the very fabric of your DNA and becomes part of who you are. Today we learn a different way to receive—and give—communications in the Kingdom. And love, the key, the answer, the way, the method, the air and breath and drink and sustenance of it all, will cover and sustain.

NEWS FLASH: Job Descriptions for the Kingdom!

The Kingdom is looking for lovers! The Kingdom is looking for lovers! There are job descriptions out and the main requirement stated is for people who love, those who are predisposed to love. Those who love love, who love to love. Individuals who don't find it a chore, a duty, or distasteful. Lovers with no agenda, no hidden motive, but just love, because the King and ruler there loves. The Kingdom is handing out flyers and wanted posters to the highways and byways, to the least "desirable" places, to the not so tasteful places, to the places where it is just not popular to be seen in some circles.

And you know what? There are many applicants. Not the ones you would have thought. Not the ones that those already in the Kingdom would have necessarily recommended. But the offices in the Kingdom are being flooded with applicants who seemingly have no qualifications, beyond the fact that they just like love. There has been so little in their lives. They have tried church, those interviewed said, but no one seemed interested in them. They had friends and family who weren't interested in them either, yet they heard that this King wasn't too particular. He would take anybody, they heard.

And something in their hearts rose up and ran ahead of them, as they ran with the flyer in their hands. When asked later, they couldn't even remember the journey or how they arrived at their destination. They just knew that the office where they arrived had welcomed them with open arms and had even been standing outside the door expectantly waiting for them to come. Those interviewed stated that they couldn't seem to get over how welcome they were, considering their meager qualifications and experience. So many others seemed much better qualified. After all, so much of their lives had been wasted while the others they observed going into the churches on Sunday morning looked so perfect for the job. They seemed holy, even. That's why they hadn't applied before. It just seemed too impossible to believe that they would even be considered.

Looking for love. That's what the poster had stated. How odd, when the King's name seemed to be Love. Why would He need more? Weren't the people He had enough? Looking for love. They wondered what kind of Kingdom could this possibly be? Even as they made preparations to join, go, or do whatever was required, they were amazed at the unprecedented way they had been treated. There seemed to be no discrimination. That's good enough for me, they all said, as the line outside the offices grew steadily longer and the people coming out seemingly both more joyful and more bewildered at the same time.

What kind of qualification was love anyway, even if it is the only one we have, they thought. Why this is unheard of in our world. This seems too good to be true, and probably it is, but we're going to give it a shot anyway. Where else do we have to go? We've been everywhere else and almost died many times, trying all the other ways. Love seems too easy. But it sure feels good. Surely it has to be more complicated than this?

LOVE IN THE KINGDOM

Though I speak with the tongues of men and of angels, but have not love, I have become sounding brass or a clanging cymbal.
1 Corinthians 13:1-2, NKJV

In the Kingdom, there is no prevailing thought, "without love." Only in the world is that phrase applicable. For in the Kingdom, since the King IS Love, the quality and strain of love abounds. It is in the very DNA of heaven. As we ponder the life of Jesus, we can see that love displayed, exhibited, and released on every level of His life. It resounded in His language and in His stance in the world no matter who was confronting Him. It caused His message to resonate with life, because love fueled it and gave it wings. No matter the sin, the degradation, or the motivation: the gentleness of Christ spoke with love. Even His anger was motivated by love. Turning over the money changers' tables in the temple, His love for the house of His Father was released in a cleansing, purifying stream.

Leaving the house of His parents at the tender age of twelve, He calmly stated that His place was to be about the business of His Father. Love drove Him to the mountainsides, to the tax collectors, and to the fishermen. Love stopped the stones of the contemptuous accusers, and set a condemned woman free. Love drew men from their livelihoods and their professions to serve the unseen Kingdom of an unseen God. Love washed the dirty feet of a weary traveler and dried the mud with a sinner's hair. Oh, that we understood the quality of that love!

Love stopped the stones

If we could only comprehend the length and breadth and depth and height of this love of Christ! Love brought Him down from paradise into the confines of hostile time and space to confront an uncaring and belligerent race bent upon destruction. Love caused Him to submit to the cruel judgments of those so much lower and with so much less power that it takes the breath away. Love gave Him the strength to endure scorn, persecution, and vicious hatred. The vileness of all that tried to destroy Him was met with only love. Violence was an unused, unthought-of avenue, as the Lord of Glory went about in peace, meeting all resistance with none of His own.

His gaze saw through to the heart, the motives, and the intentions of all He met. The indifferent masses were stripped bare at a glance from the eternal eyes of the Son of God. But mercy, identified with love, triumphed and ran with the colors of this new champion, for just so is He. He is our champion, the One set into the fight on our behalf. He fought all the angry hordes both in earth and heaven, for us, all because of love.

He is our champion

His tenderness and love was extended to the lowest, the most vile, and to the smallest and most insignificant. The children flocked to this One Who could have called on unmentionable power at any moment in His earthy sojourn. He was a traveler, sent from another place to exemplify from whence He came, with love, love, and more love, until Love gave His life. His enemies, jubilant, considered Him a defeated charlatan, and rejoiced in the storm following the cross.

For His Kingdom is not of this world. His love is not either. The world's ways and the world's understanding do not apply and cannot measure the caliber, density, or dimension of this kind of love. Dictionaries can't define it. Scholars can't research it. Preachers can't find the oratorical words to express it. It is the love of the Father, existing from age to age, immortal, unchangeable, and freely given. It is the love of the Kingdom, and the essence of its life.

THE MAJESTY OF THE KINGDOM

The chief characteristics of the Kingdom mirror those of its King. While acknowledging that this King is invisible and eternal, still we must recognize that many of those who people this Kingdom are currently inhabiting physical mortal bodies. How then do we reconcile these two seemingly opposite standpoints, and still clearly define and come into alignment with the attributes of the Kingdom?

> All Your works shall praise You, O Lord, and Your saints shall bless You. They shall speak of the glory of Your kingdom, and talk of Your power, to make known to the sons of men His mighty acts, and the glorious majesty of His kingdom.
>
> Psalms 145:10-12, NKJV

From this scripture we see the glimmers of something not yet completely discerned, but longed for and imagined. Some have even been granted glimpses of it. But how shall we define majesty? Could it be found in the rounded cheeks of a child as he expresses his pure joy in living? Is it to be seen in the grateful murmur of the hungry as they are fed, or in the shy recipient of love extended which has been all too rare in his life? Who can price kindness, generosity or the laying down of a life for others? Who can put words to the splendor of selflessness or the radiance of humility? Where does greatness lie if it is not in Christ's hand extended to those in desperate need through willing Kingdom dwellers?

When in search of majesty, generally one pictures it as munificent wealth, in gems and glittering raiment or in great beauty and stunning grandeur. We as human beings tend to define according to our previous experience and our well world-trained perspectives. But the Lord's thoughts are not ours, nor are His ways.

Love is the Key

So again we must realize, *Love is the key*, and all of its off-shoots the root. This is what unlocks the heart. Love is what develops and seals the unbreakable bond that forms the Kingdom. This love is the incomprehensible, unknowable splendor of the nature of Christ the King. This love forms and fuels the fires of the brilliance and the light so sung about, taught about, and spread abroad throughout the world. Yes, *Love is the key*. Love is the key to the definition of the majesty of the Kingdom.

Where is the heart that bursts forth out of its fullness to minister to the helpless? Where is the soul so transformed by Jesus' love that it rests in the wait, while longing to serve? Where is the one who has crucified all of his ambitions to lay them at the feet of the Master, willing to change his course and directions at one small word from his King? Where is the one waiting in the shadows, on the sidelines, unnoticed and unsung, content just to be ready knowing that his destiny is in secure and omniscient Hands, and that his days are numbered and his times sure? Where are the servants, running here and there without regard for person or future, thinking only of the tasks at hand which lighten the loads of another?

Where are the quiet ones, the restful ones, the full-of-wisdom ones who hold fast God's sure and present Word, like apples of gold in settings dripping with of silver? Where are the joyful, bubbling with the surety of faith and dripping with miracles, not the miracles least of which is this very joy?

These ones are the marks of the majesty of the Kingdom of Heaven. These are the majestic ones, the ones who shine forth with the splendor of their Maker. These are the ones who illustrate the majesty of this invisible realm. These are among the many who represent Him clearly. Their resonance is like clear pure bells ringing out the sounds of an eternal spotless realm where love abounds and true majesty resides.

The Wealth of Kingdom Majesty

Like a great and deep river, the wealth rolls on, very unlike worldly wealth and the antithesis of earthly visions of beauty. And everywhere this water touches, even one drop, the dead live again.

> But there the Lord will be for us in majesty and splendor a place of broad rivers and streams, where no oar-propelled boat can go, and no mighty and stately ship can pass. For the Lord is our Judge, the Lord is our Lawgiver, the Lord is our King; He will save us.
>
> Isaiah 33:21-22, AMP

Who can define this life, this power, except to say that its splendor is like the sun shining in its strength? This light is so bright that it dazzles and blinds world-weary eyes, though they could not see anyway. Even as children must be taught not to stare into the sun, earthlings must be taught to peer into His majesty with God's eyes, applying the eye salve that HE provides (Revelation 3:18), in order to acclimatize the mortal gaze to the immortal.

For this majesty, this splendor, this light, is immortal. It is supernatural. It is unearthly. It is outside of the bonds of time and space. It is therefore beyond our own boundaries and farther than our earthly reach. It is out of our control and untouched by human emotion and will. It is ever broader than our conception, even while we make baby steps toward the comprehension of our God. This glory is earth resistant, anger repellent, and certainly pride retardant. All of the machinations of man's intellect cannot affect, infect, tarnish, nor alter in any way the intrinsic nature and value of this indefinable glory substance of the Kingdom of the living God.

Our mistake, perhaps one of our greatest, is that we continue attempting to intellectually understand. And in failing to do so, we pass on by to those things which we are sure that we do understand. But to miss this glory! To be blind to this splendor! To be imprisoned by our own perception and our own human thinking! The thought of this causes such pain that from our innermost being bursts desire: Oh, that this God of power would stoop to our lowliness and lift us up to Himself, that we might be one with Him. That we might share in His glory, be bathed in His essence, and be changed into His likeness.

But to our amazement, we find that this then is the very crux of the nature of this majesty: that He chose us for His own and has made this very thing to be our destiny. He has chosen to bestow upon us comprehension and even alignment with this boundless love, this matchless grace, and this forgiveness so full and free. And so, transformed, we may peer not only into this glory realm, but become aware that it is all around us, and our eyes are ever opening wider to see.

This is the season to see, to really see. If only we have the courage to look! For we must look not at the things which we have seen, but at the things which are not seen and eternal (2 Corinthians 4:18). Transfixed, we are beginning to gaze into the matchless, full of wonder, deep, flowing, Life-current Majesty of the Kingdom of Heaven. And with eyes of child-like wonder WE SEE.

Kingdom Alignment

THREE

Discerning the King

So often when we think of royalty, a sort of star struck mentality intrudes on our perception. Common mores and long held beliefs have become our mental structure with regard to a king or queen, the princess or the prince. They are apart from common mortals. They live a fairy tale existence, without the common worries and everyday mundane details of the working man's world. That's why they are so revered and followed. Just to glimpse, just to touch what they have touched, just to have an autograph and we feel that we have contacted another world.

We don't want to know about their everyday lives. We don't want to know about their struggles, lest it detract from their persona. On the other hand, some hunger after the human, ordinary details. Somehow in knowing about the ordinary, the royals seem less removed and more a part of our lives. Either way, we delight to live their lives vicariously, from a distance, something to worship from afar and idealize as part of the imaginary haze in which we prefer to live.

The royalty of the Kingdom of God is another matter entirely. The ineffable truth which so permeates the very air of the Kingdom insists that there be neither haze nor deception about THIS royalty. Indeed, all of the known, written, inspired Word as set forth in the Bible has basically one purpose: to make the King known to His people. "Come unto Me, all ye who labor and are heavy laden and I will give you rest." Jesus was all about coming to Him, not about staying away and keeping a proper distance and declaring, 'revere Me but don't touch.' Sadly, many of His ambassadors, advocates and intermediaries have taken the world's view of themselves, and not the persona of the King

Himself.

But as we explore the Word of God about our King, we find that this King of ours is as far removed from the earth's luminaries "as the earth is from the heavens" (Isaiah 53:8-9). In every way possible this is the literal truth. He is NOT of the earth. In no way does He resemble the fallen earthly hierarchies and dignitaries. That is the reason our spirits are so grieved when the heads of churches and ministries begin to resemble, even in small ways, the rock stars, movie stars and human idols of our world. This is not the nature of God. This is not the DNA of God. This is not the indwelling heavenly protocol of the Kingdom which is not of this world.

Truly, we are receiving revelation on high to finally DISCERN THE KING. In learning Who He truly is, we learn more fully and completely who WE are, and how we are to live in this hour and for all the eternities ahead. We are not about just surviving in this world, although riding triumphantly through it and all of its difficulties is certainly part of the life of a Kingdom dweller. We must be about aligning with the King of all Kings, and learning to reign with Him. This is a difficult thing to do if we don't know Who He is and cannot comprehend even part of the fullness of His LIFE.

Discerning the true nature of the King and becoming totally aligned with Who He is, is a vital and crucial component of today's agenda. How can we properly align with His Body on earth, if we don't know Him and therefore are not in alignment with all that is close to His heart? "Oh that I may know Him, and the power of His resurrection" (Philippians 3:10).

This longing was put there by the divine, that we might search Him out, wading through and out of the world's perspectives into the clarity and purity of divine thought. What a challenge that lies before us, and what a higher call and more divine purpose! Focusing on the higher, loftier, and more complex yet simple truths of all existence is the command of the Lord.

into the clarity and purity of divine thought

...whatever is true, whatever is worthy of reverence and is honorable and seemly, whatever is just, whatever is pure, whatever is lovely and lovable, whatever is kind

and winsome and gracious, if there is any virtue and
excellence, if there is anything worthy of praise, think
on and weigh and take account of these things [fix your
minds on them].

Philippians 4:8, AMP

As the pure seeps into the complex morass of our humanness,
gradually all within us is shaken up and we begin to eject the impure,
leaving crystal clear depths within. Like the clear streets of gold in His
city, we will begin to have firm foundations on which to walk, and
clearer, more illuminated steps ahead of us. For you see, in the Kingdom,
all paths and directions are illuminated by the Lamb's lamp, and there
is no need for maps and GPS coordinates to guide us to our destination.
This is aligning with the King and His thoughts.
This is aligning with the Light, and through *illuminated by*
this process, becoming the Light. *the Lamb's lamp*

THE LIGHT OF THE WORLD

Jesus, the Light of the world and the Daystar, is the exact
representation and extension of all that God the Father is. He is the
bright and morning star, rising in the darkness of the night sky with
the sure and pure shining of hope eternal. He is the sole expression of
the glory of God, the Light-being, the out-raying of the divine; and He
is the perfect imprint and very image of God's nature, upholding and
maintaining and guiding and propelling the universe by His mighty
word of power (Hebrews 1:3a, AMP, author's punctuation).

His brightness was like the light; He had rays flashing
from His hand, and there His power was hidden.

Habakkuk 3:4, NKJV

He wraps Himself with Light as with a cloak, and the dark and the
light are the same to Him (Psalm 139:12, AMP). Indeed, since He *is*
light, there is nowhere to hide from Him, and there is nowhere He is not
present. "In Him was Life, and the Life was the Light of men. And the
Light shines on in the darkness, for the darkness has never overpowered
it [put it out or absorbed it or appropriated it, and is unreceptive to it]"

(John 1:4-5, AMP).

God our Father is the omnipotent One, the One with all power over all the works of the evil one: all power over all darkness, and He has given us the same power. What a wonderful day when Jesus spoke to the disciples and told them that they would do even greater works than He has done (John 14:12). How can this be? Because God is for us! Since He is on our side, there should be no fear whether it is light, or whether it is dark; whether it is calm, or a storm be raging; whether we are persecuted or we are honored; whether we are despised, or loved. He covers Himself, and us, with light.

> Bless the Lord, O my soul!
> O Lord my God, You are very great:
> You are clothed with honor and majesty,
> Who cover Yourself with light as with a garment,
> Who stretch out the heavens like a curtain.
> He lays the beams of His upper chambers in the waters,
> Who makes the clouds His chariot,
> Who walks on the wings of the wind,
> Who makes His angels spirits,
> His ministers a flame of fire.
> Psalm 104:1-4, NKJV

"I am the Light of the world," Jesus said of Himself (John 8:12). And as His light shines upon us and upon our world, we must have greater understanding of the nature of true light. This light is not merely artificial yellow light designed to light a small area before us. This light is ALIVE. This light is not light which we can understand. The light of this amazing King is the true light, which all other lights emulate. What are the characteristics of true, supernatural light?

"Light not only exposes and deposes, but it proposes. It's like a courtship. Light would woo us, beguile us and entreat us. Light would exhort us, encourage us and uncover us. Light is not threatened, defensive or apologetic. Light is friendly but unequivocal. Light is impartial but not always 'fair.'

Light is frank, straightforward, and dependable. Of course it reveals the Truth. It never lies, and never desires to lie. It never desires to skirt around whatever it reveals or whatever it finds. It just IS. It has in it the perfected ability to abide, just as we should abide in the vine. So the light abides. It doesn't prevaricate, circumvent, or manipulate. It enhances beauty, and reveals joy; it brings pleasure and gives strength. It has the ability to cause man renewal of purpose. It has the ability to stir man to greater effort, greater achievement, to greater fervor and zeal.

perfected ability to abide

This Eternal Light is very clean and pure. It is almost laser in quality, in that it will beam into its object and bore with such stunning purity that flesh cannot stand it. It hates it in fact. So if we would press on into the Light, if we would press on toward the mark of the high call of God in Christ Jesus, Who is the Light, then let us band together as soldiers of the Light, arm to arm, rank upon rank, shoulder to shoulder. Let us band together and march into the light, carrying the banner of the Cross. Ever before us, the Cross of the crucifixion of all of the works of darkness."[2]

This Light Being, this triune God of power, will have no need to cloak His might or soft pedal His message. In the Kingdom of Heaven, the very light and might that can be so destructive in the fallen earth will be the way of operation, a normal day with Him, as we move in the realms we were designed for. The fire that seems so fearful will simply be the release of the authority of the King in the greatness of His love.

As His messengers and His servants, and also as His Bride, we are moving into another realm of the understanding of the authority extended by that famous scepter. We are not only the recipients, but the extenders as well in this Kingdom which is not part of the earth. Becoming aligned with Him is more than we bargained for. It is more than we asked or certainly than we were able to think. But without fear, we are responding to the call of authority,

Come! Come up here and I will show you....

Let me show you! Don't you love the phrase! Not, I will hide and see if you can find Me. But, in a voice ringing with power and love and authority, Come and I will show you! How can we not respond? How can we apathetically go on in the way we always

persistent door-knocking King

---

2   Paragraphs from the author's work, *Overcomer: The Emerging Church of the Third Day*

have and ignore the most exciting invitation in the universe? He shows us things to come and He shows us things past. He reveals present realities, wisdom choices and illuminated scenes of heaven. He is a REVEALER. He is a persistent, door knocking, seek-you-out in the highways King of Glory. Has there ever been such a King? Has there ever been such a Power Light Being so compassionate and kind and full of love?

This is the most exciting person ever alive in the cosmos. His is the greatest intelligence, the most massive creative force, and yet the most generous and humble nature imaginable, moving and running upon the hills and valleys of our world.

In our quest for understanding the triune God, we also look at His enemies. There is a saying, "A man is defined by His enemies." God is defined solely by GOD. His enemies, full of bluster and self-importance, have a certain following. Deception blinds even the Lord's servants and they sometimes become unwitting allies with those forces seeking to undermine God's hosts. But justice will prevail. The Kingdom is advancing and routing Satan and his friends. One of the central themes in the Kingdom is His victorious army, overcoming the evil one and setting the captives free.

LORD OF HOSTS

A great general, the Captain of the Lord's Hosts is commanding the Mahanaim (the "army of two companies," Genesis 32:2) and great masses both in heaven and in earth are moving into place for the battle of the ages. Not that it is called that because it will be so difficult, but because it will be so glorious, so astounding, and so thrilling to watch the defeat of the hordes that have been causing such torment and agony across the spans of time.

Defeat and victory!
Defeat and victory: the great defining of the King.
This is who He is, One Who reigns!
One Who conquers!
One Who leads the masses to their overcoming destiny!

This is our King! He has so many facets, like a diamond shining in its splendor, He is the mighty warrior. The Ancient of Days on the throne with emerald rainbows surrounding. He is the gentle Shepherd and the foot washing Servant.

Our triune, omnipotent God is drawing the ages to a close. Time is coming to an end and all its confines with it. Strictures and structures are falling away as the earth prepares for its final conflict. The changes we see are the moving into place of all creation.

The great steeds of the Lord are pawing the ground, snorting with impatience! We were made for battle! Let us go and let us run! Rising up within all of us is the restlessness and impatience that precedes great change. Let us focus on our Leader, as He rides into the fray! Let us follow in His wake, shouting already at the coming victory! What exhilarating challenges lie ahead for the triumphant residents of the Kingdom! Angels are preparing the celebration as the kings of the earth rage and further the tumultuous melee.

we were made for battle!

All of the earth will celebrate the Lord, and the trees of the fields will clap their hands before the coming of His great majesty. And so we, the lovers of the Lamb, will focus on the things not seen, and allow the seen to swirl unheeded and un-feared around us. The King and ruler of our Kingdom has made this possible for us. You see, He is the possible-making God. He thrills to do the impossible. He delights in challenge and doesn't hesitate at the roar of the enemy; He is a mountain moving, death defying, darkness stultifying God. His might rides upon the very obstacles before Him, using them as stepping stones to fly even more swiftly forward.

> Gird Your sword upon Your thigh, O Mighty One, with Your glory and Your majesty. And in Your majesty ride prosperously because of truth, humility, and righteousness.
>
> Psalm 45:3-4, NKJV

His wisdom, lent so sweetly to Solomon, counsels the great, while His peace runs ahead, calming troubled waters. Although storms arise at His presence, His voice calms and brings life to all around Him. This is such an important part of His nature: the innate ability to bring life out of death every time. With Him, life is always the result. His desire is to restore, transform, and to heal. And His joy strengthens us in the midst of it all.

ONE WHO LAUGHS

Have you known His joy? It is our glory, and the lifter of our head. It is a mighty river running through us, sometimes a bubbling brook, and at other times a deep and strong tide, bearing us ever, ever upward. Being borne upon the ocean-deep river of God is to be carried aloft past all the trials and traumas of life, always with that constant pulsing of joy unspeakable and full of glory.

> You will show me the path of life; in Your presence is fullness of joy, at Your right hand there are pleasures forevermore.
>
> Psalm 16:11, AMP

Joy is in the birdsong at first light and the call of the thrush and the nightingale and the creatures of the field in the darkness. Joy is the sight of the shinings in the heavenlies beyond the feel and the smell of the despair of this world. Joy unites all in a common love, a common purpose and a common destiny. Joy is that which provides the impulse to put one step in front of the other, laughs while we do it, and applauds as the trials go past. Joy is the fresh smell of Jesus-rain in the air that will cause the peoples of the world to cry out, to hunger for, to desire, and to long for the receiving of the next smallest word from the One whose joy is our strength.

fresh smell of Jesus-rain

Truly, our King is one who laughs. Wouldn't you love to hear what must be a full-throated thunderous rumble, free and unrestrained, causing all of creation to quiver in delight? That very laughter can unleash the terrible might of this powerful One, causing His enemies to flee in terror before Him.

Somehow, the thought of that laughter is a trust enabler. This is One to be trusted. One on whom to lean. This is a Father to the fatherless and a refuge in the storm. This is One to run to and be enclosed, enfolded in the everlasting arms. This is the lover of my soul, my guide and stay; my keeper and shepherd, the One who fills my cup.

Whatever my need, He is there before I call. This is my God, the One in whom I trust.

BELOVED

There are so many layers and levels and depths to this amazing Being who will spend eternity with us as our Bridegroom King. We cry with the words of the Apostle Paul, Oh, that I might be able to comprehend the love of Christ, which passes knowledge! Oh that I might know Him!

Space in this small book cannot begin to capture or explain the fullness of who He is. But the most wonderful mystery of all is that He has chosen US, He loved us first, and He desires union and communion with us. He desires our attention and treasures our love and desire for Him. "Draw me after you and let us run together! The king has brought me into his chambers" (Song 1:4a, NASU). Truly, He is our Beloved and we are His.

This King sparkles with Light as a diamond of many facets and superb cut. This King, even in the midst of His glory and splendor, has a care for the smallest and least significant of His creations. Full of wisdom, He rules with justice and mercy. Gentle and kind, His humility brings Him to honor the lowly. Steadfast, He endures patiently, with fresh lovingkindness, new every morning. True *militantly on our side* and pure, He sees the end from the beginning and waits for us, knowing our thoughts and yet militantly on our side anyway.

He will never leave or forsake us, He will never disappoint or fail us, and He died that we might live. In His infiniteness, Jesus Christ our King allows us in our finiteness to attempt to discern Him. He allows our scrutiny, even requests it, knowing that as we contemplate Him, the Spirit of wisdom and revelation will reveal His Person to us. We will become ever closer and closer to Him, until we are transformed into His image, from glory to glory.

> So shall the king greatly desire thy beauty: for he is thy Lord; and worship thou him.
>
> Psalm 45:11, KJV

Holy and sweet communion between the Bride and her Beloved bursts into a new realization as each loved one reaches new closeness and vulnerability with the King. The Lord's drawing and wooing of our hearts will produce in us a longing to not only experience, but to dwell in a place we could call the rain of tears. Most would be reluctant to accept such a concept, dismissing it as emotional. But the tight reign we have kept upon ourselves, both emotionally and spiritually, has often restrained us from receiving the tenderness of His love and grace inside of ourselves, in the greatest places of need.

We will allow all of our inward walls to fall in the vulnerable experience here in these encounters with our Beloved. We will trust completely in Him as He enters our heart, touching us with His Holy Presence so deeply that weeping is the result. As we release ourselves into this comforting place of unfamiliar tears, there will be a dissolving of inner deceptions and misplaced perspectives. Clarity always comes after rain.

This rain of tears is a place destined by God to be a refuge for those who hunger and thirst, desperately desiring His Presence. But He is drawing even the most prosaic, pragmatic, and hardened thinkers to a place with which they are most unfamiliar. They will not find intellectual comfort here, nor satisfaction. This will be new territory, a new journeying, and the silver rain will fall all around. From the inside of the most rigid of believers the rain will fall, and also from the outside, where many others will be caught up in a corporate move of the Holy Spirit in this place of tears.

The cleansing of this welling up will wash away the crustiness of years and the callousness from the wounds of so many arrows. Once one is yielded and yielding, the hard knots of tension, grief and bitterness inside will dissolve and wash away, never to be seen again. The rain of tears: this is the place of grace. For there is coming a fresh baptism of His grace and this grace will be an explosive releasing and destruction of the dam holding back the storm and rain: the rushing outward of pent-up waters of life within every hungry heart.

Enter within this new veil, misty with the unknown. This release will help to catapult the Beloved of the Lord into a new level of experience in His Presence which has been longed for but not yet touched. The release of the rain of tears, the release of grace, and thus the release of His Presence and sweet communion with Him, is our destiny in this hour. He is our Beloved, our King, and His heart seeks after us.

I sleep, but my heart is awake; it is the voice of my beloved! He knocks, saying, "Open for me, my sister, my love, my dove, my perfect one; for my head is covered with dew, my locks with the drops of the night."

Song 5:2, NKJV

Kingdom Alignment

Four

Peoples of the Kingdom

You are the God who performs miracles; you display
your power among the peoples.

Psalm 77:14, NIV

Who Peoples the Kingdom?

The magnificent I Am, Creator of the heavens and earth and our
great King, is continuously calling for whosoever to come into His
Kingdom. But somehow the question remains, who can actually come?
Who is allowed? The exclusivity ingrained in us by the world compels
us to inquire once again, for it is difficult to fathom the total inclusivity
of His loving call. Who fits the criteria?

Who has, besides perhaps love, the qualifications? The elite, the
leaders, the authoritarians, the scholars, and the professionals, these
qualified without question ones are understandable. But who else, and
how does He recognize the eligibility of those who are to come in?
This may seem a ridiculous question. But who, indeed, peoples the
Kingdom?

And those who heard it said, "Who then can be saved?"
But He said, "The things which are impossible with men
are possible with God."

Luke 18:26-27, NKJV

The answers are found throughout the Word of God. His call goes to the thirsty, the weary, and the heavily laden. In fact, He says, quite simply, that whoever calls on the name of the Lord shall be saved (Acts 2:21). How different from our world! We tend to worship at the altars of the famous, wealthy, and the ones with "power." But according to scripture, Luke states that the Kingdom belongs to the poor!

> And solemnly lifting up His eyes on His disciples, He said: Blessed (happy, — with life-joy and satisfaction in God's favor and salvation, apart from your outward condition — and to be envied) are you poor and lowly and afflicted (destitute of wealth, influence, position, and honor), for the kingdom of God is yours!
>
> Luke 6:20, AMP

It is quite evident that the invitations sent out by the King are myriad and infinitely non-exclusive. His heart looks in the darkest places, in the most remote, surprising, unlikely and even undesirable locations unfrequented by the elite. None are turned away. None. A repentant heart is the only qualifier to entering this prepared place. "The time is fulfilled, and the Kingdom of God is at hand. Repent, and believe in the gospel" (Mark 1:15, NKJV).

> For God so loved the world, that he gave his only begotten Son, that whosoever believeth in him should not perish, but have everlasting life.
>
> John 3:16, KJV

Salvation from a world of woe, sin, degradation, and ruin. How simple it sounds, almost too simple. Can years of fear, depravation, hatred and any number of earthly prisons really be wiped away in a moment? Absolutely! Will they be remembered, kept in a file, and referred to if one "slips up?" Never! Because sins are cast into the sea of His forgetfulness and new creatures are born every day, sprung out of the morning, dipped whole into the dew of His grace, and changed forever.

dipped whole into the dew of His grace

What is the Sea of His forgetfulness? It is the place where all that is not born of Him that had attached itself to us goes to lie forever, forgotten and securely frozen into annihilation. It is only the carnal mind of man that tries to revisit, resurrect and bring it back into being, aided by the powers of darkness. But God's forgiveness, so full and free, is given and never taken back. He is not a man to lie or change His mind. He does not give, only to take away in some humanlike fit of pique. Only our choices can change our fate for the worse. God's choices for us always change our direction and circumstances for our good.

> And we know that all things work together for good to those who love God, to those who are the called according to His purpose.
>
> Romans 8:28, NKJV

Yes, all may come and all are welcome. There are no entrance fees, dues or score cards. In His Realm is found grace, mercy, loving-kindness, and redemption. Think of it: abundant affirmation, edification and encouragement. In His Kingdom the welcome find the Spirit Who lifts up and Who crowns with glory and honor (Psalm 8:5). This is His desire for Kingdom people.

Who can come? Who is welcome?

You! And you, and you!

The Kingdom of Heaven is peopled by many, many groups of varied, unexpected people of infinite variety, a colorful boisterous mix, never boring, and all different. Their purposes are multi-layered and faceted, all necessary though non-competitive, making the texture and sounds of the Kingdom so thick that, like the Word of God, the depth of it can never be found.

His Voice

The Kingdom is peopled by anyone who hears the sound of His voice with that simple imperative, Come! Not selective, it rings through the hills and across the valleys, down the mountains and through the desert. His voice runs faster than light and larger than sound. It is ever seeking, searching the lost one, the forgotten one, the rejected, the wounded and the dead.

His voice, the thunder of His voice which pierces through darkness like the most refined laser, that voice demands an answer. It disallows death. It isn't guided by reason or humanness of any kind or shadow. Supernatural, it pierces, cuts, stabs, and bores through. It is unstoppable, unshakable, not timid or tentative, but imperative, forceful and full of power. It is the Voice of the Lord.

> And behold, the glory of the God of Israel came from the way of the east. His voice was like the sound of many waters; and the earth shone with His glory.
> Ezekiel 43:2-3, NKJV

What can one say when one considers a subject as vast and unknown as the voice of the Lord? For His voice, like His nature, is sung about, taught about, and studied, but rarely experienced in this realm in its fullness. But scripture tells us that this voice is so powerful that it causes birth to come, that it shakes the earth, and makes His enemies tremble (Psalm 29). This voice is like the voice of the lion, the king of the forest. When he roars, his enemies are paralyzed and his prey is left at his mercy.

The terror of the voice of the Lord causes the mountains to melt and yet gives ease and comfort to His Beloved. There is a timbre in this sound that is recognized by all who know Him. "My sheep hear My voice, and I know them, and they follow Me" (John 10:27, NKJV).

His voice demands that we follow. Within us resonates a harmony that instantly answers and follows, even though we may not understand. His *woos the reluctant beloved* voice sings in the midst of the congregations and woos the reluctant beloved who hides behind the lattice (Song 2:9).

When He plays upon the strings of our hearts with His magnificent thunderous rumble, all that is within us melts just like the mountains, and we become changed. The glory of Him Who rides upon the deserts Has Spoken! One wonders whether we would survive in the desert that is left without the sound He makes as He walks within His garden (Genesis 3:8).

When we stray away from Him, it is the memory of His voice

that woos us back into the place of sweet communion. For this is the moment longed for. This is the hour cried for in the night seasons. This is the shining, piercingly sweet instant of eternal change: the moment of communion with the King of Glory. All that is within us needing to be shaken is dislodged and annihilated in this time of awe, this time when the Almighty speaks and we hear.

The voice of the Lord calls to those destined to be peoples of the Kingdom, and they thrill to answer and follow. The voice of the Lord rings with the strength one needs to answer. It shakes and disintegrates all resistance, as His beloved moves to respond. The revelation of the ages drips from it and guides all into the Truth sought after, the Truth unsought, and the Truth which sets the prisoners free.

All prisoners, all captives, all the tormented, pained and rejected, the voice of the Lord is calling you to your appointed place of freedom and rest. Listen without fear! Hear without apprehension and skepticism! The voice of the Lord is calling, calling; He is calling you into His Kingdom! And you will know your place, and you will accept it with joy.

People Groups in the Kingdom

The ultimate creation of His Majesty and His greatest joy was man. He made him to be unique, not only from the rest of creation, but He created him to reproduce in uniqueness, in developing creativity, as man learned to fashion himself after his Maker, the great Creator. And so man learned to create, and to be creative, and to multiply and be fruitful, just as he was commanded in the beginning.

In this creativity, man himself became a fascinating, complex organism, with many facets and infinite variety. The infinity of God began to be dispersed throughout all mankind, and the joy of God continually rejoices in this colorful display of His own nature.

Are there people groups in the Kingdom? Somehow it is unusual to conceive of people groups when one discourses about the Kingdom of Heaven. But in the Kingdom these are not people groups as the world would define them, and they do not follow the world's criteria. Only God knows the massive lists of assignments, tasks, heart descriptions, and other designations of these wonderful ones. Only He might "group" them in His heart in delightful, unusual, and deep ways.

HIDDEN ONES

Let us speak of the Hidden Ones of the Kingdom. These are the closeted ones, the ones unknown and unmentioned. Hearing the call, they came, and so they remain, faithful and stalwart, quiet residents of His own. They are shut away from the adulations of men, from the fame, the press, and from the "favor" of even the world weary Body of Christ. These are the crucified ones, every day, in every way.

These are the ones without a "name," the ones who labor in the vineyards of the Lord tirelessly, making a difference, making life in the midst of darkness, and making a way where there seems to be none.

death is a
way of life

These are the ones who die a little every day, to their own ambitions, to their own desires, and to their own ways. To them, death is a way of life, not the death of the wicked one, but the selfless death of the One who conquered death, hell and the grave.

> That I may know Him and the power of His resurrection, and the fellowship of His sufferings, being conformed to His death, if, by any means, I may attain to the resurrection from the dead.
> Philippians 3:10-11, NKJV

Yes, He left an inheritance of death. He left an inheritance of darkness to the ways of the world. He left an inheritance of suffering, castigation, and persecution. This must be received with the rest of the Kingdom riches. For this is wealth; this is the true wealth of the Kingdom. This is the fellowship of His sufferings. So few ever find it or truly understand it. They lose their way in fame or riches, even in the favors of men, though well meaning and lavishly bestowed. This favor leads to death also, but not the death desired by the Holy One of Israel.

He has explored the various kinds of death, and conquered them all (2 Timothy 1:9-10). He knows in His infinite wisdom the labels of men and what lies behind. He knows what lurks in the darkness of the minds of men as they complete each day's struggle for a good word, an encouragement, or a sign that someone notices and recognizes their worth. It is the eternal search for approval.

So where are these who cry out in the darkness at the injustice of the world's thinking and the world's scale of choice? Have they survived the place of crucifixion? Have they overcome the rejection and the silence, or the lack of affirmation of their peers? What of the ones in the remote areas where that is not even an issue? They are the ones who labor unseen, unheard, unknown, unsung, and unnoticed by those who "matter."

The Darkness of Obscurity

Is this the true Kingdom life then, to rest in obscurity? To rest in whatever state one finds oneself, knowing that He, the crucified One, will exalt whom He chooses. Those who truly rest recognize this truth: He exalts and brings low, and in His will they will rest with rejoicing and thanksgiving. The grace of the Kingdom is there to cover all who labor in obscurity, for theirs is the Kingdom of Heaven. Blessed are they who are pure in heart, and poor in spirit, who glory in their weaknesses and rejoice in their infirmities. Where is the true wealth of this unseen realm? Where are the hidden treasures, the secrets of darkness, the hidden place of the stairs?

> And I will give you the treasures of darkness and hidden riches of secret places, that you may know that it is I, the Lord, the God of Israel, Who calls you by your name.
>
> Isaiah 45:3, AMP

He directs His own into all Truth, and ever leads and guides those in the Kingdom whose portion it is to dwell in the darkness of obscurity away from the strife of tongues. They will rest with grace and thanksgiving.

> You shall hide them in the secret place of Your presence from the plots of man; You shall keep them secretly in a pavilion from the strife of tongues.
>
> Psalm 31:20, NKJV

Can these perhaps be ones who see more than others, who recognize the guises of those in the limelight, and who are not fooled by the masks of the fame of this world? For the corruption of fame and wealth would attempt to erode the very structures of the Kingdom. And who is more surprised when there is no effect on that eternal structure? For, like so many other areas, the carnal motivations and manipulative intents of so many, however unconscious, have no effect on that which was not made by human hands

Peace for the Hidden

Oh pilgrim, rest well in your obscurity, for the darkness is as light to Him who made you in secret and Who wove your innermost being before the foundations of the world. Know peace, oh troubled soul, who cries out in the night seasons for the living God, and who waits in impatience for one word, one breath, even one sigh from Him whom your soul loves.

Torment is not always from the evil one. Many times the worst pain can come from those who would call themselves your friends. Time and again the most agony would come from those who simply ignore the gift of God within you, or who don't recognize the hand of the Holy One upon your life. Be at ease, oh troubled one, for you were called by Him, anointed by Him, gifted by His design, and sent out in His plan and for His purpose.

In His Kingdom your approval does not depend on the reactions of others, even those in great and high visibility. Your affirmation is from Him and Him alone. You only hurt yourself when you seek it elsewhere. Look only to Him, seek only Him, judge yourself only by Him, and only He will direct your steps and destiny. Trust Him that every step has been ordered and directed in His perfect will. Trust Him that He is

Only Him able to complete that which you have committed to Him against the day of the Lord.

> And He has made my mouth like a sharp sword; in the shadow of His hand has He hid me and made me a polished arrow; in His quiver has He kept me close and concealed me.
>
> Isaiah 49:2, AMP

Be encouraged, your destiny is secure. Do not measure it against the world's standards, which have intruded into the areas of the Kingdom most visible to the world. A great shaking is coming, greater than ever before. Many ungodly and evil activities and people will be exposed, and many innocents vindicated. But what is vital and important is that the peace of the Most High God keeps your hearts in rest in the midst of it all. What seems most impossible will be the most possible in this seemingly upside down realm which you have entered.

Don't try to understand; don't try to measure this season by past standards. Don't be troubled by those who continue on in their "comfortable" old ruts, swaying the masses with the undulations of charm and charisma. For the purity of the Lord is upon us. Repentance is the key. Repentance will free you from the prisons this season would weave around you.

Remember that nothing you are experiencing did He not first experience. He bore it all. He saw it all before it happened. He is not removed from you, and He is not far away. He is near you, even in your heart and in your mouth. Don't search for Him in the fire and the whirlwind and in the experiences of others. Search for Him with all your heart in the innermost recesses of yourself, for it is within you that the safety of the Kingdom dwells (Luke 17:21).

> In peace I will both lie down and sleep, for You, Lord,
> alone make me dwell in safety and confident trust.
>
> Psalm 4:8, AMP

This is the unfolding and fulfillment of the great mystery of the ages: He is in you, all of His love, His mercy, His forgiveness, His grace, and all of that power and strength. He is inside you, waiting to help, to love, and to aid. It is not as complicated as you would think. Breakthrough is coming and more will be made clear than you ever dreamed. This life as you know it will change, but you will rejoice in the change, knowing that His plans for you are for a future and a hope (Jeremiah 29:11).

There is great hope ahead that will reach out and grasp you, strengthening you for the times ahead. And the Presence, that Almighty Presence, will cause you to lose the fear of obscurity, of failure in the world's terms, and the nightmare of non-accomplishment. This

Presence which you have sought so desperately will sweep away all of your previous fears, anxieties and doubts.

So many things will wax dim before the great Light that is shining. Watch, wait and expect this Light. For this is the season of Great Light. This is the season of great and overwhelming joy. This is the season long awaited, that will liberate the hearts of men and cause acceleration to propel you onward into new climes, new vistas and new experiences. This is the season of breakthrough. This is the season of the Kingdom.

the season of the Kingdom

THE BURDEN BEARERS

There are many in the Kingdom who could be identified as Burden Bearers. They support, lift, and carry unseen loads, loads most people are unaware of and don't understand. It is difficult to find compassion for those recognized as burden bearers, since they labor for invisible reasons which even they may not fully comprehend. Burden bearing would not qualify as a mission that receives accolades and applause. The implication of bearing burdens and the effort necessary to accomplish the task is not a popular concept. People are most familiar with their own identifiable burdens, borne daily with much stress and labor.

The Lord says to cast your burdens upon Him and He will sustain you, for His yoke is easy and His burden is light. In the Kingdom, the weight of the burden, spiritual or earthly, is borne by the Lord. We might carry it, but He bears the weight, the strain, and the load. If we allow Him, for it is always our choice, He will carry the heavy burdens as we labor and tarry with Him.

"Come to Me, all you who labor and are heavy-laden and overburdened, and I will cause you to rest. [I will ease and relieve and refresh your souls.]

Take My yoke upon you and learn of Me, for I am gentle (meek) and humble (lowly) in heart, and you will find rest (relief and ease and refreshment and recreation and blessed quiet) for your souls.

> For My yoke is wholesome (useful, good-not harsh, hard, sharp, or pressing, but comfortable, gracious, and pleasant), and My burden is light and easy to be borne."
>
> Matthew 11:28-30 AMP

It is interesting to note that the Greek word for rest means "intermission," even suggesting "recreation." So often we labor unnecessarily, always weary, looking everywhere for ease, but we do not find it because we never look in the right place. That recreation, that intermission from stress and labor, is found in Him, and in His Body.

In the Kingdom we are yoked together, aligned with each other, and always, ever, with the Lord. He never assigns something too difficult to bear, too heavy to lift, or too wearisome for His children. His is a gentle, loving nature, one which seeks to lift rather than to burden down. The severity of the human condition is not found in the heavenly climate of the Kingdom. Ease is there, and peace, but never that driving, insistent frazzle oriented, guilt producing constant prod.

So many of us are dragging around, pulling heavy baggage that we were not designed to carry. Burnout is a common problem today, and is the fault of that to be laid at the Lord's door? Are there misunderstandings somewhere in the perception of which orders came from heaven, and which did not?

Clarity must come as we consider new order and structure in this day of change and repositioning. The clouds of past misconceptions and actions must be dissipated by the new winds. The fresh winds of the Spirit are calling for differences in perception, and certainly in fresh ways of hearing divine orders.

Divine Burdens

It must be remembered that the burden of the Lord is a divine burden; therefore it cannot be viewed as the world might look upon a burden. The burden that Habakkuk saw, or the one released by Ezekiel: these are the burdens which were given and borne to bring life to the people of God. The motive and intent of today's burdens must always be identified and discerned by Kingdom people. Which burdens are human, and which divine?

It is hard to imagine what the giving and receiving of the divine burdens of old felt like. Can we put ourselves in the shoes of Paul, Jeremiah, or John the Revelator, when that divine call came, and with it the burden of the Lord? Can we imagine the divine light, the breathless wonder of that haze, or the desire for the next and the next and the next, once the wondrous weight of heaven's burden has been experienced?

Truly again we must acknowledge that it is the worn and rutted man-roads in our brain that cause such agony when we think of bearing yet another burden. But a voice from heaven is calling for new definitions to come to bear in this new world. What is the definition of "burden?"

> The burden of the word of the Lord for Israel, saith the LORD, which stretcheth forth the heavens, and layeth the foundation of the earth, and formeth the spirit of man within him.
>
> Zechariah 12:1, KJV

The Hebrew word used here for burden is 'massa', meaning something carried, an utterance, and indicates a reference to singing. In scripture we read about Ezekiel's burdens (Ezekiel 12:10), the burden which Habakkuk the prophet saw (interesting word in Habakkuk 1:1), and the burdens of many of the other prophets. These as the Lord's burdens were not human, wearisome onerous tasks. They were supernatural, "like fire, shut up in the bones" (Jeremiah 20:9).

Bearing the burden of the Lord is a divine call to carry the Word or the heart of the Lord for His season and purposes. It is the Lord's voice calling often in the night seasons when we feel that weightiness in the Spirit to receive the burden of the Lord. And so, with His strength, we receive it, and go with Him in prayer, releasing it as we partner with the Holy Spirit and often with the groanings which cannot be uttered (Romans 8:26-27).

Releasing the burden with ease is as important to consider as the receiving of it. Whether a burden in prayer, a prophetic burden, or an assignment in governmental staff or position, we are often so accustomed to carrying our load that we are reluctant to let it go and move on. Trust was required when we accepted the present assignment, and trust must be applied to allow us to relinquish it.

The weary find it harder to remember that it is a divine burden. Those about to faint with the heaviness of the tasks at hand cannot properly wait upon the Lord to renew their strength. They go by rote, day by day, without hope of change and without joy to fuel their stamina. So many today sigh at the thought of another burden, another task, and another schedule filled day.

The Kingdom of God has a different kind of life, and a different kind of burden. Perhaps it is time to take another look at the burdens presently occupying our lives, and assess if they are indeed divine. In His Kingdom, there is hope of deliverance from drudgery, doldrums, and the plodding existence so prevalent in today's workaday world.

> Who is this King of glory? The LORD strong and mighty, the LORD mighty in battle. Lift up your heads, O you gates! Lift up, you everlasting doors! And the King of glory shall come in.
>
> Psalm 24:8-9, NKJV

While one still goes to work to pay the rent and all of the other demands and obligations of life, the King of Glory is on His throne. He is assuring us that hearts were created to be light and full of joy, carrying the flame of life from another world into the work place, and the marketplace, and into all the corners of a world still trying to be as Godless as possible. The burden bearers of the Kingdom are light bearers! They are flamethrowers! They are runners, carrying the baton for their segment of the race!

It is time to undo the heavy man-made burdens and let the oppressed go free. It is time to pick up the burden of the Lord instead, thanking Him for the privilege, and running ahead in the sheer joy of it. Burden Bearers of the Kingdom are chosen of God and trusted by Him to complete the assignments of the invisible realm of power, and to walk comfortably in the unknown! Lion-hearted, they move with courage and in His immeasurable, divine strength. Like their King, they boldly forge ahead with the authority and confidence of those on a divine mission under sealed orders.

Lion-hearted in divine strength

Burden Bearers are only one battalion of the varied peoples of the Kingdom, that great and vast multitude of many peopled, many featured and gifted ones called of the Holy One of Israel.

Another group one might consider is one which the world identifies by gender. Much ado has been made in the world and also in the church over the "woman question." What is the Lord's heart regarding this interesting group of people?

CAN WOMEN BE ALIGNED IN THE KINGDOM?
A Prophetic Message to the Church

"Concerning the equality of women I would discourse, says the Lord. Equal to what, I would ask? Equal to whom? From whence would this comparison spring? Does it come from God's throne, and from His thoughts? Does it come from His enemies, the more to confound? Does it spring from religion's claws, or tradition's reaches? What is the source, what is the root of this most violently argued question? For the debates have echoed through political rallies and voting booths, through school halls, and among the church pews. This point of argument has bounced back and forth between old and young, through many races and cultures, and in many homes and families throughout this great earth and across many eons of time.

It is such a hotly contested issue, such a foundation for tears, recriminations, fisted fights, and stiff-necked opinions. For surely I am right, says one. But my stance is the only perspective, says another. This is the way it will be, expounds one sect, and these are the rules and boundaries, decree the leaders of countries. This issue, this seemingly elusive truth, has plagued mankind surely since the proverbial apple in the distant beginning of all things, both good and bad.

There are answers, and one truth to be found, if only a questing pilgrim were to give up everything to find. For that is what it requires, says the Lord. Give up all of your carnal intellect, all your opinions and all of your need to be right, and God's truth is easily found. Seek, and keep on seeking, and you will find, says your God. This truth, like any other, has its deep roots in Me, says the Lord.

Let Me ask you a question. Where is My love for My people? Have I set it on one alone? Have I preferred one above the other? Or did I die for all? Did I come to set slave against master, or Gentile against Jew? Then neither did I come to set men against women, says the Lord. For I came to bring together, not to set apart, I came to restore and heal, not to put one in bondage under another. For I am bringing the high low, and the low high; making the crooked straight and the rough places plain. I come to loose the heavy burdens and to let the oppressed go free.

Into My Kingdom prejudices of any kind will not enter, for the greatest will be the servants of all. The high and lofty will be uncomfortable in the Kingdom of Heaven, for humility will open the front gates and service will demand honor.

The kingdoms of the earth would set races against one another, and class, and gender as well. But there is no such thing where I dwell. Those who are nearest to Me and hear My heartbeat will remember ALL of My servants, My judges, My prophets, and they will know that it was always the willing that I chose, not the lofty and not the proud. It was the courageous and the ones who loved Me, and not the one of color, race or gender.

Did I not come to bring liberty to all? Did I not set the women free? Did I condemn, punish, or subjugate? Did I isolate, imprison, or harm? Was My love not freely given to all? And did I not deliberately choose the weak and foolish things of the earth to confound the wise?

For I will not bow to the manipulations and rationales of men and I will not nod and wink at their excesses and the twisting of My words. The polarization and alignment that is coming upon the earth will bear My stamp and My seal. It will bear My mark and My name. The foundations, boundaries, and structures of My Kingdom are set in My truth, with My nature and My character their identifying mark.

My peace has come to destroy prejudice. My joy has come to needle and torment the mean-spirited religious judgments plaguing My Body. My fire has come to purge, purify and cleanse the temple of all that is not of Me, says the Lord. And as My glory rises, one will hardly remember why they preferred one over another, or accused Me of doing so as well.

In the alignment of My Kingdom, there will be neither Jew nor Greek, bond nor free, male nor female, and My government shall be of My own choosing. Allow Me to choose.

stark, razor clear exactness of the Word

Let My wisdom rule and My grace abound. Let My Word prevail and My preferences stand alone. Allow humility to bring your mind-sets down, until what is in your mind is the stark, razor-clear exactness of the Word of God, living and active, piercing and exposing.

Learn to choose to be exposed. For when you lose the fear of being exposed, you will find that what is left is My glory in you, shining for all to see. Prejudice must fall before the blinding rising of My Light. As My thoughts rise within you, the splendor and clarity of My mind will set you free from the torments of human thinking. The freedom of this will take your breath away. The rigidity of the everyday struggle to continue with so many opinions will soften and melt away before the enormity of My love.

My love will align My entire Kingdom, every race and tribe, every kindred and tongue, every created one of My desire, fitly joined together, unified in My covenant. I am a covenant keeping God. And My covenant is for all, freely given, and freely received.

It will surprise many whom I choose and which will hold what position. For I do not choose as man chooses, and I will exalt and bring low, even as I continue to redeem, deliver, and create. Did you know that your opinions and mind-sets limit and slow the creativity of the King? As you release all of this to Me, you will discover the true creative nature of your King, pulsing in your blood and racing in your veins.

Come and run with Me! Come and fly with Me! Leave the ground-hugging, dirt-eating lowly ways of the earth's thinking, and fly with Me on the wings of the wind! You are only limited by your thoughts. You are never limited by Mine.

Prejudice is not My way. All are welcome and equal in this new world. Let the old things pass away, for the new, like My lovingkindnesses, are fresh every morning. Enjoy My mercy and My grace. Look for your space, for it is here, waiting for you in My Kingdom, in My paradise, in the place which I have prepared for you, says your God."

There is neither Jew nor Greek, there is neither slave nor free, there is neither male nor female; for you are all one in Christ Jesus.   *Galatians 3:28, NKJV*

THE COVENANT BROKERS

As we consider the peoples of the Kingdom in this limited space, we have mentioned only a few. Although short, this list must include a final group in our current study, one we might call the Covenant Brokers.

One cannot consider the Kingdom of Heaven without pondering one of its most important and prominent characteristics: that of Covenant. It is fact that God is a God of Covenant. We know that the details and terms of this covenant were clearly laid out by His hand to His people throughout all the centuries of His plan.

Who would guess that so few really understand or abide by this amazing and binding heart issue. We must know, however, that as members and residents in this eternal Kingdom we are bound in cords of love to the same heartbeat of our King. And His heartbeat is one of covenant.

The agreement and set of divine promises between God and His people known as covenant is recognized as one of the most important theological truths of the Bible. Unlike a contract, which always has an ending date in the time schedules of man, a covenant is a permanent arrangement, an eternal divine contract. It does not refer to one or two aspects of God or man, but refers to the whole being: all of God, and all of man. Since God does not break promises, His covenants are sacred, beyond human invention or intervention, and everlasting.

The Ark of the Covenant

At one point in the ancient times of greatest transition and God-training, the Father directed the children of Israel to follow what was identified as the "Ark of the Covenant."

> So it was, after three days, that the officers went through the camp; and they commanded the people, saying, "When you see the ark of the covenant of the Lord your God, and the priests, the Levites, bearing it, then you shall set out from your place and go after it.
>
> Joshua 3:2-3, NKJV

To the Israelites the ark was considered to embody the Shekinah presence of Jehovah. The name, Ark of the Covenant, signified that this mighty incomprehensible Being had made a binding and everlasting promise to them which He called "covenant." They were commanded to follow the Ark, no matter how hard, no matter how foolish it seemed, and no matter how they felt about it. This covenant and command to follow are still fresh and active today.

In this present day, we are called to remember, watch, and follow this covenant God and His incomparable Presence, as He prepares to release continuing revelation of the power of the covenant. We entered this realm of covenant when we entered the Kingdom. We are only now becoming more aware of all of its ramifications as the light rises on this new day. Nothing in our past can help us in laying hold of the future. But as we focus and follow the covenant, we will come into greater release of this unimaginable source of power: the power of our covenant with God!

> Until the Ancient of Days came, and judgment was given to the saints of the Most High [God], and the time came when the saints possessed the kingdom.
>
> Daniel 7:22, AMP

The Power of the Covenant

A time is coming when the saints will realize the power of the covenant, and begin to possess the Kingdom, with all of its privileges, graces, and power. As residents who focus and follow as commanded, power is immediate. All of the wonders of our God are ours and instantly available. His covenantal promises have bestowed upon us all that He is. "Love has been perfected among us in this: that we may have boldness in the Day of Judgment; because as He is, so are we in this world" (1 John 4:17-18, NKJV).

Some in the Kingdom have revelation of this shining, immaculate, pure, and sacred vow. They walk in the light of this truth, shedding its power abroad as they go. They are advocates of God's Promise, this Oath of our everlasting Father. They are negotiators with the world. They literally "broker" for the covenant. They argue its merits. They explain its privileges. They reveal the path to entering in, and they mediate and stand between, until those who are lost and blind can come and can see.

The Covenant Brokers lay down their lives for the Truth. These special emissaries don't care for their own lives, but live for the power of the promises of a covenant-keeping God. Talking to one is talking to the King, so accurately do they represent Him and His purposes. For His purposes have become their own, and His heart theirs. They lie awake in the night and plan and listen and plan, so that every effort will be divine, and every outcome and glory His.

You won't find a label by their name, or a plaque on their door. You won't read about them in the newspaper, or find their direction in a brochure. They don't fit into the usual designations; in fact, most wear many other hats in the Kingdom, and have varied duties. But deep in their hearts they consider their most important destiny to be God's agent, illuminating and unleashing and demonstrating the great power of the covenant.

Are you one of these? Are you one of these quickened, awakened saints who possess the Kingdom and its covenant power? Are you one whose heartbeat would reveal the King and Him only? Can you leave all that you know to follow as directed into much that you have never seen? Are you willing to go where you have never been before, so that others may find the way? Can you lay down all of your ambitions and desires to further His?

Are His oath and bindings of love more important to you than the pleasures and promises of the world? Are you focusing and following that covenant, paving the way for others though you may never see them or hear their acquiescence? Is this Kingdom and its covenant-keeping God more important to you than your own life? Are you a Covenant Broker?

Destiny Redefined

The moment is upon us of redefining our destiny and who we ultimately are. The labels of yesterday are so limited beside the boundless revelation being poured out upon us in this present season. Defining ourselves will only limit our horizons. Allowing those around us to define who we are will narrow them painfully.

We are being aligned and re-positioned onto higher ground and broader places of abundance. We belong in the Kingdom, but our designated positions are changing as the Kingdom and all of its peoples slowly mature and move into their realized destiny. May the Omniscient One open our eyes to those around us. Not as we have known them once, but as He sees and knows them, and as He continues to design and even elaborate on their unique, matchless, and wonderful nature.

The peoples of the Kingdom are realizing their destiny! They are multiplying their graces, gifts and authority as they submit to the cleansing purity of the King. He is purging, purifying, and glorifying the peoples of His Kingdom. Let us align ourselves with all that He is moving upon by His power, and watch as that which we have never seen materializes in glory before us.

FIVE

The Alignment Principle

Did you ever feel that you just didn't fit in? I did. I was tall growing up, taller than most everyone. I made good grades. I played the piano. I constantly went to church. With these combined attributes, I just didn't fit in with my other classmates. It was painful, humiliating and uncomfortable not to "fit." I never seemed to be in line with everyone else.

To compensate, I spent a great deal of time choosing flat shoes and slumping down trying to minimize my height. I longed to be included, although I didn't really grasp what that would feel like. I never considered my overall future and what acceptance would mean to my life. I simply knew that I wanted it.

From time to time, I have physically encountered issues with my back. Various physicians murmured words like "out of alignment," and we all acknowledged that this was not good. "Out of alignment" generally meant "in pain." It gradually followed that "in alignment" meant "out of pain."

As I began to study the Kingdom of God, I found much the same principles in operation. Often those learning that they are "in" the Kingdom have virtually no idea what this means. Currently in the Body of Christ, perceiving the mystical Body and apprehending true knowledge of being aligned together is a difficult pursuit if, at the same time, one is being rejected or ignored by most fellow "alignees."

The Body must learn it is a cohesive unit, inseparable from all the other parts and learn proper behavioral patterns to fit the reality. In this awaking perception of "in alignment," we can happily eliminate much of the pain that being "out of alignment" may have caused. We begin to recognize that ALL can and have been coming into this place where we are learning to dwell. We are "thrown together," and a great lining up is taking place.

This principle can be seen in the global awakening and shaking across denominational lines as well as in the various religions of the earth. Polarization is happening, like it or not. Alliances are being made in many arenas and on varied fronts. Convergence is rearing up, with almost catastrophic results.

In the natural world, disasters and wars dominate the news. Alignment is beginning in every kingdom, some with wars to insure the intended outcome. At what point will the kingdoms of this world become the Kingdom of our Lord? Which kingdom will we be aligned with when the process of transformation begins to manifest? And concurrently in our recognition of where we are aligned, how can we respond in an appropriate manner?

How can all of these whosoevers, these varied multi-faceted and differing individuals fit together or align with one another? How can it be expected that people meet together in any way, when before, it was never possible in this world?

TOGETHER

Kingdom alignment must occur in order for the next phase of victory for the church to continue. In such a critical and even dangerous time, the army of God cannot win unless they are *Together* and *Unified*. God's army must come together, aligned for His purposes, and aligned to assure the foundations of the nations. The forces of God must be aligned and positioned for the great coming out of the Kingdom. A vast inaugural party is scheduled. If unified and properly aligned together, we all can take our place with joy in the celebration banquet.

A net designed to hold fish cannot work if the separate pieces are not closely and securely joined together. In like manner, the Kingdom must be rightly and securely linked together. The great plan of the enemy is to separate, divide, and conquer. Be assured, our enemy will conquer if we are not together. A house divided will NOT stand. Unfortunately, division is taking place more quickly than anyone may have anticipated.

Recently many of us were in shock after a national event, questioning for days, how could this happen? Even now, questioning continues and if we simply keep repeating it, this focus could cause us to join the losing side in the war for our souls, lives, and our way of life. Much of what happened was caused by lack of unity and alignment. Kingdom people must pick up the threads of lost unity, and present a united front towards the enemies of our way of life.

threads of lost unity

Kingdom alignment must take place so that the ultimate plan for the building of the Kingdom can move on to its next phase. There is great difficulty in building and waging war at the same time; however it is not too late for significant and rapid progress to be made. Awakening must happen and there must be a great coming together. The word alignment suggests a lining up, a getting into place, and an ordering, which is required for maximum strength to be released. This concept can only be realized if we are *Together*.

The Kingdom is rising out of the mist like a giant monolith, one of its great strengths that nobody knew it was there. Protected by its very obscurity, it is now manifesting and we are beginning to see the release of its power. If we want to be part of this rising, part of this triumphant positioning and advent of Kingdom dominion, we must come *Together*.

triumphant positioning

The Power of Unity

Many parts of the Kingdom have been operating at some level and with some power, but greatly hampered by the fact that they were not rightly connected in their assigned portion of God's Kingdom. Like a room in a building wired for electricity but not connected to a breaker, many vital parts of the Kingdom have been and are inoperable, simply because they are not interconnected, they are not *Together*.

Much like a ship listing to one side because one section has become logged and filled with the very substance it was destined to ride above, the Kingdom has been infiltrated with the very world that the King warned we were not to be a part of. This infiltration or contamination causes the unthinkable: disunity in a government designed to be run, operated, governed, enjoyed, and empowered by the people: *Together*.

Sooner or later we will become increasingly tired of the lame, powerless sham or pale shadow that the church is evidently attempting to become, instead of its very real and vital design by the Most High God. How cruel to be only a shadow when we are designed to be the LIGHT. How devastating to be a shell when we are designed to be the ideal, the matrix, the example, the WINNER.

Unity Broken by Separateness

So many members of the many-membered Body feel cut off. This is because many are. They are not separated by the design or decree of the King, but by their own choices, whether conscious or unconscious. Bitterness, rejection, jealousy, rancor and ill will in the individual parts have caused rifts in large sections of the Kingdom.

Like a magnificent custom designed mansion created by a famous architect yet lying vacant and unoccupied, so also are large areas of the Kingdom. Lack of alignment has caused isolation, free agents, unhealthy independence, and rebellion. Sadly, even hatred and schisms exist in what should be a unified realm of unconditional love. Refusal to come together or to work together has caused vacancy in what should be the most occupied and powerful unit on the face of the earth.

There is hope that the situation can be rectified. It is not too late. We can still participate and assist in the coming of the Kingdom. Remember who is King. He is the God of the impossible. He is the God of miracles. He is the King of glory. He is the power source. He is our Redeemer, who takes the inoperable and the ineffective and the impotent; He takes the failures and despairing Has Beens and in a moment, just the twinkling of an eye, He can cause resurrection of purpose and power. He can bring us together, in re-life-ing, revival reformation. He can reconcile and calm the violent storms and troubled souls.

resurrection of purpose

Love never fails. Love is the song, the refrain, the air of the Kingdom. Love can recall, return, and re-attach the prodigal, heal the lame, the paralyzed, the leper, and indeed, even the greatest failures of our time. Watch for this love. Watch restoration of those whom you never thought to associate with again. Be willing to be reattached to a severed limb, a dark and lifeless eye or a gangrenous finger.

Because the Lord, our King, the One who doesn't need or require our vote, is making a decree to bring the Body back *Together*. He knows all that we do not, because He is the King. He is the Lawgiver. He is the Sage, Judge, and the Righteous One, Who is all the things we are not in order that we can become the things we are destined to be. He will enable us to live together forever as members of a mystical, spiritual, authentic Government of *Government of* Eternal Ages, world without end, in this amazing *eternal ages* realm known as the Kingdom of Heaven.

Resign yourselves to it. Yield. Desist. Give up. Give in and JOIN TOGETHER. Become a vital part of today's Kingdom connections, working and laboring, all equal, all important, and all healthy. Together we have a common goal with none preferred, sharing the task of harvesting the fields of the Lord. Together we lighten the load of every individual part, giving each small piece the opportunity to be bigger than it could ever be alone, with infinitely more accomplished. Together we will be effective and strong, each part determined to hold onto the other with the manifestation of the Spirit for the *common good* (1 Corinthians 12). Let us covenant to work together in unbroken unity.

> Simon Peter went up and dragged the net to land, full of large fish, one hundred and fifty-three; and although there were so many, the net was not broken.
>
> John 21:11-12, NKJV

KINGDOM CONNECTIONS

For a number of years a good friend of mine has had a ministry entitled Kingdom Connections. What a prophetic, illuminated and ahead-of-its-time name, for that is precisely what God is about in this hour. He is making the separate members of the Kingdom CONNECT in the way that they must in order to meet destined timelines. Kingdom alignment is ALL about connecting.

All kinds of ministries have been birthed and growing in the last few decades. These ministries and their leaders must begin to work together with common goals and purposes in order for GOD'S purposes to be made manifest. God is bringing about Kingdom connections in order to bring us into a season of the rain of fire.

> Surely His salvation is near [ready to be appropriated, below] to those who reverently and worshipfully fear Him, and is ready ["may dwell"] to be appropriated that the manifest presence of God, His glory may tabernacle and abide in our land.
>
> Psalm 85:9, AMP

As we work in the vineyards of the Lord, the presence and glory of the King are to be our common goals while preparing for the greatest harvest the world has ever seen. We sang an anointed song many years ago, "Bind us together with cords that cannot be broken." In this day and hour, we must be bound together with love. The love of the King must bind us together, in order that the synergy of all can *transport the fire and power* needed to win a dying planet to the Lord.

Connections of Power

Some years ago during a prayer meeting, I had a vision. I saw what seemed to be an electrical grid, intricately woven together and stretching over the earth and through infinite space. It was much like an electric blanket without the blanket material, and obviously created to be plugged into a power source of some kind. As I waited, the Lord spoke:

"There is a connection being made. I am connecting the Kingdom. I am connecting structures that have been in their place for centuries. The power grids are completed. This is a season of connecting the grids. The Light of the World is being seen as power grids across the globe discover and turn on the power destined.

Watch, wait, look and listen, for I have done My work and I have listened to My people. Now the manifestation of that which was prophesied of old has come. Darkness has covered the earth, and gross darkness covers the peoples, but upon them a great light is shining. Watch, wait and listen. For sound and light are partnering and a great alliance has been negotiated in heavenly realms as the crust of division is broken and heaven manifests in earth. Watch, wait and listen, for I am doing it in this hour, says the Lord."

The alignment coming into the Kingdom today is creating a massive unit that works by power. The Lord is connecting each power source already laid, one to another. It is a power grid. It is alive with the dunamis power of God, with an electrical charge that goes through every link. It is not a dead or lifeless organization made by human thinking. Unlike the nets of the disciples, it is an electrified, alive net made to catch the hearts and souls of men so that the glory of God can dwell in the land!

Oh, hallelujah! We are grateful! We are grateful to God in this hour that we aren't dependent upon our own limited strength. We can plug into the luminous power of the Holy Spirit as the power grids of the Kingdom are being connected. The manifestation of the power and glory of the Lord must be seen in every part of the Kingdom.

Darkness and the Light Power of the Lord

As I thought about the Kingdom as a great power grid, I realized that grids like that are so interconnected that when one part goes out, it takes out whole blocks in the grid with it. And so for the entire Kingdom to be empowered it is vital that all of the Kingdom be connected, receiving the power source together. For the entire Kingdom to be empowered, the entire Kingdom must be networked together for transformation. Together many links create a massive power light. One small link would provide tiny light, while an entire power grid would provide massive light and power to combat the darkness.

Several years ago, I was hosting one of our conferences seeking the Presence of the Lord and revival. It was held in a large church where the sanctuary was lit solely by artificial light, having no windows. After the first song during one of the services, suddenly all the electricity in the church went out. Great darkness seemed to envelope us. The electric instruments could not play. The entire sound system obviously did not work. We instantly became very aware of the power of light, and the overwhelming challenge of darkness!

We began to sing and praise the Lord. A light gleamed faintly in the back of the sanctuary. I looked from the stage toward the center aisle, where I saw a young woman coming, carrying a lighted seven branched candle stand. The lights of the candles gleamed softly in the darkness. We could not see ourselves, our instruments, or even one another. Everything but the Lord became obscure outside the short range of the flames of the candles.

The Presence of the Lord and the Spirit of revelation began to envelope us, and we prophesied and sang the word of the Lord for three hours. Prophetic music sang His heart and His power, the violin, flutes, trumpets and drums playing heavenly harmonies. The electrical power of the Lord was in charge of the service!

At the end of the meeting, the sanctuary still lit only by candles, I led a time of a cappella worship in an almost breathless Presence of the Lord. When I ended the closing prayer with Amen, instantaneously all the lights came back on. The timing was so startling that the people screamed, shouted and applauded.

What we were not aware of until later was that a city transformer servicing a radius of six miles had gone out. The entire block of the electrical grid where we were located had lost power to the source! But almost the most amazing part of all was that the circuits were repaired in this large area of the city in an hour or so, and thus the lights in the rest of the church had come on some time earlier. This greatly perplexed the church staff, who couldn't find out why the lights were not on in the sanctuary as well, since they were on the same switch as the rest of the church.

The natural electricity in the Lord's meeting did not operate until He designated it so! What a demonstration of the importance of connection to the power source both natural and spiritual! The Lord of Light is bringing focus to bear on His great power, and upon the lights of the peoples of the Kingdom that are beginning to shine into the darkness of this present age with more and more effect and brightness. They are casting their brilliance in obedience to His direction and His purposes, handling His great power with grace, ease and love.

It is academic that a conduit carrying massive electrical current must be insulated. God's love is the insulation of His great power! Without love, people can be injured. So in this time of the releasing of power and light, there must be new building codes. We cannot build the way we have in the past. It won't work. The structures aren't big enough, far-reaching enough or strong enough. The purposes of God are different than the original intents of the men involved, therefore change must come. God's plan is unfolding and we must change the building codes!

My husband and I once lived in a small house that was wired in 1950. I can't stress this enough: That was an electrically challenged house! I had extension cords all over the house. I had signs taped everywhere, "light switch to back porch" (not on the back porch), and "light switch to hall" (not in the hall), because the light switches were in all the wrong places. There were switches we never used because we couldn't find out what they were intended to light. These were labeled "light switch to nowhere." Jesus is not coming back for an electrically challenged Body!

TRANSFORMATION

Each church and ministry has a part in the infrastructure of God's power grids. All are intended to be plugged into the overall power design of the Kingdom, with the whole in direct contact with the head of the Body, the King. A great focus of the power of the Kingdom is for the transformation of the earth. The beginning of the church was clearly marked by the power of God.

> And seeing signs and miracles of great power which were being performed, he was utterly amazed.
>
> Acts 8:13, AMP

Transformation requires great power, and it requires both the Head and the Body. This is an important principle, seemingly hard for many to grasp. The power can't all be in the Head. The Body has to have the same dimension and the same level of power as the Head, because the Head and the Body are one. We have a dysfunctional Body of Christ, when the Body isn't doing what the Head is doing, and certainly not with the same level of power. It requires both the Head and not just parts of the Body, but all of the Body, working together. Unity brings great power, anointing, and thus transformation.

TRANSFORMERS

In any electrical grid, there must be transformers in place to take the energy and transform it so that it can be used by everyone. Transformers are connectors of electricity; they take the power source and do mysterious things with it and then disperse it out to the many so that it can be used. The fire and energy of God is meant to be usable by all, in every denomination, in every stream, and in every church. God is raising up leaders, redeemers, evangelists, and preachers as *handling the power*

75

fire starters and transformers.

But transformers must themselves be transformed before they can fulfill the purpose of handling the power. Like Moses, we must have a burning bush experience. Not once, not twice, but every day we must seek out the power source! Transformers must be transformed before they can ignite the rest of the world with the fire of God.

Transformers must see as the First Transformer, our God the Consuming Fire, sees! Saul of Tarsus was transformed before he had the ability as an apostle to convert a heathen people into the church that harvested the world for centuries and never died. Transformation calls for the leadership of the Kingdom to continuously release the great explosive power of the unleashed and unhindered without measure LIFE OF GOD, in earth as it is in heaven.

God's desire is transformation that will never die, revival that will never pass, and transformation that leads to reformation. His purpose is reformation that will cause every blind eye and every deaf ear to see and hear. He will have a grateful, healed and transformed radical Body of believers full of passion.

KINGDOM ALIGNMENT

The Kingdom is destined to work together in unity, functioning clearly as the explosive power of the unleashed, unhindered, without-measure life of God. The world will see a strong, healthy, unified, electrified Kingdom in place and in time, for the common good of all.

The peoples of the Kingdom will be rightly fitted and aligned together. They will be aligned with their King, knowing Who He is, hearing His heartbeat, and inseparably joined to His purposes. This Kingdom of Purpose will work in and display His undiluted, uninhibited out-of-this-world power, and the manifested glory of God will tabernacle and dwell permanently in our earth.

> Yours, O Lord, is the greatness and the power and the glory and the victory and the majesty, for all that is in the heavens and the earth is Yours; Yours is the kingdom, O Lord, and Yours it is to be exalted as Head over all.
>
> 1 Chronicles 29:11, AMP

Six

Governmental Alignment

As we seek the revelation of the Holy Spirit concerning the development of this powerful and glorious Kingdom, we can clearly see the unfolding of the Lord's plan over many centuries during the expansion of Israel. The Lord continued to reveal Himself to His chosen people. He revealed Himself as King, Lawgiver and Judge. He taught the people to fear Him, yet at the same time He was teaching them of His love and tender care. As the Lawgiver, He set up structure and clear governmental principles for His chosen people for their time.

The natural kingdom of Israel was a shadow and standard for the spiritual Kingdom yet to be revealed. The power, the glory, the light, and the government were present, but only as a shadow of what was to come. As we watch shadows, we can partially visualize the real in movement and shape. Watching natural Israel was just so. But a great revealing was coming, and the Lord was a faithful King. God loved His people unconditionally and laid out His plan patiently and methodically throughout centuries to come.

With the coming of Jesus the King, the Kingdom of Heaven was proclaimed to be at hand. Things had changed. The shadow was dispersed by the sun, and a new covenant had come.   Instead of a fearful nation and the mysterious God who came as fire on the quaking mountain, there is a mystical "Body" of believers, with Christ as the Head and King over all. So the principle of government and alignment came to take on new definition, at the same time that everything else began to change.

> For unto us a child is born, unto us a son is given; and the government will be upon his shoulder. And his name will be called wonderful, counselor, mighty God, everlasting father, prince of peace.
>
> Of the increase of his government and peace there will be no end, upon the throne of David and over his kingdom, to order it and establish it with judgment and justice from that time forward, even forever. The zeal of the Lord of hosts will perform this.
>
> Isaiah 9:6-7

GOVERNMENT IN THE KINGDOM

As great changes escalate in challenging the earth, the Body of Christ, and our way of life, our focus wisely turns to the Word of God and the invisible, immortal realms in which God dwells. But living here in this physical earth, it is wise that our attention also dwell on the practical, everyday walking out of this Kingdom as it continues to increase, manifest and grow in the power of the Holy Spirit.

In these next few chapters, let us turn our attention to these practical issues, which march alongside the revelatory and prophetic dimensions in understanding the Kingdom. The way we walk and structure these practical areas in churches and ministries can either greatly hinder or do much to facilitate the expanding of the revelation and illumination breaking with great light upon our horizons.

Practical Workings of New Covenant Government

As the Lord laid out governmental structure in the light of His New Covenant, He speaks of apostles, prophets, evangelists, pastors and teachers. Ephesians 4 provides us with a profound and strategic moment in history. As Christ Jesus ascended from the earth, He left it with a blueprint for government, manned and vitalized by His Body here— a mystery!

Many ages have passed as the Church expanded and grew, and governmental concepts and principles expanded with it. Through this expansion over the centuries, the Church experienced various human applications in governmental formation that challenged the foundations of God's plan. Excesses and abuses hindered the moves of God as well as the healthy growth of His people.

The deep joining together of this shining Kingdom must evidence at its core the unity of an unshakable and heavenly governmental structure reflecting and propagating the nature of the King. And so the question continues to resound, how can man govern the masses of the mystical Body of Christ known as the "church" with the eternal wisdom and nature of the King?

Today in many of the streams and denominational designations of the church, there is a widely accepted belief that leaders are a type of governmental "covering." This term has come to reflect concepts of government with regard to authority and submission. One of the major controversies from church history emerged as a result of the principle of shepherding and covering. While that initial movement is in the past, many church governments still practice the same general principles. What is the truth in this important issue?

Churches are often said to be governmentally covered by apostolic networks or denominations. However, covering and submission to these overseeing groups are continuing issues of debate. The principle of submission is indisputably present in God's word. It seems that our interpretation of the Word of God concerning submission and covering is the cause of so much of the conflict.

It is recognized and necessary that there exist in the Body of Christ today, leaders, ministries and organizations who provide accountability, protection and guidance to one another. Many offer it as a ministry in itself, a service to the Body of Christ. But much confusion still muddies the water as we define boundaries and search for some sort of rule book in a matter that, while alluded to in the Word in various applications, is often sadly at the mercy of broad opinions and interpretations.

Often systems set up for the common good are flawed but typically bear up under scrutiny. This is necessary for the overall purpose of oversight to succeed. The truth is that we need one another. Society and history show us that as we find our places together in groups and systems, more is accomplished; we can become more, grow faster, and individual opportunities are more readily available. Loose cannons and lone rangers have no safety nets, no accountability factors, and no support systems. In attempting to be "independent," they can become over-exposed, drawing attention to self and thus becoming a potential target for criticism and possible failure.

The great Kingdom of Heaven operates in the same excellence of structure and ingenuity of design as does all that God administrates,

excellence of structure and ingenuity of design

both visible and invisible. In every organization there must be leaders, decision makers, and generals, as well as regiments of those who implement the blueprints and designs. There is great safety within organizations and organisms that have proper Godly oversight.

SAFETY IN RELATIONAL ALIGNMENT

There can be safety in relationships, whether with one another, with leaders, or also between leaders and other leaders. The Kingdom is the fortress of our God and the place of safety prepared for us, with the accountability and oversight of governmental structure within it. To those who continue to resist these structures, we must make the obvious statement: This can be very positive! All of us need safety nets and fresh and objective viewpoints. The apostle Paul spoke of this clearly when he wrote:

> Obey your spiritual leaders and submit to them [continually recognizing their authority over you], for they are constantly keeping watch over your souls and guarding your spiritual welfare, as men who will have to render an account [of their trust]. [Do your part to] let them do this with gladness and not with sighing and groaning, for that would not be profitable to you [either].
>
> Hebrews 13:17, AMP

We are not meant to be alone. There can be relief and peace in knowing that there are others who watch, with the Father's care and love, over our souls. We are not alone. Insisting that we can do it alone is not only dangerous, but it opens a door to self-deception. You can't be part of a "Body," the Body of Christ, and be alone. We are connected, whether we like it or not, whether we acknowledge it or not, and whether we choose to function within it or not. The healthiest, least stressful, and most productive direction we can take might simply be to identify those places where we fit together and receive that relationship with joy.

Great strength comes when the synergy of the Body of Christ is allowed to reach its full potential: people, churches and ministries functioning *together in unity*. Alignment, with the proper arrangement of leadership in the right spirit and within the right boundaries, can bring about wonderful relationships and results. As we grow and mature in a healthy environment, we no longer need to hide nor put up walls around our hearts. We become more transparent and vulnerable as we learn the value and reward of trust.

synergy of the body

Vulnerability keeps hearts soft and teachable. There can be pain in that, but whether we like it or not, pain is the ultimate sign of life. Immaturity wants to correct, but mature and seasoned oversight ministries seek to restore. Jesus, our Shepherd, "restores our soul." In His stead, human shepherds can and must do the same.

When sin entered Adam's world, he lost the covering of the glory of the presence of God. Suddenly he felt naked, and physical covering became the outer symbol of all that he had lost inwardly. The Lord immediately began the plan of redemption from sin, and through Christ and His Body, a new revelation of "covering" and alignment has taken place.

We recognize the power in God our Father as He loves, gathers, covers, and supports through us, His Body here on earth. How can we cooperate with these principles that are a part of His very nature in light of the new covenant and the Kingdom?

FIRST THE NATURAL: PHYSICAL BODY

In our study of Kingdom alignment and healthy governmental relationships, let's look at the spiritual Body of Christ and its alignment functions through the analogy of the physical body. Using this analogy, the skin of the physical body can be likened to the governmental oversight ministries of the Body of Christ, with all the other necessary organs and inner working members of the body functioning in their places and fulfilling their purposes as well.

Just as the physical body is covered by skin, each part of the Body of Christ is aligned, covered, connected with and grown into, certain parts of the oversight, governmental, five-fold, equipping ministries which are set into place and given by God. So all of the spiritual "skin" (governing ministries) and all of its connected functioning spiritual bodily organs, tissues, and everything that make up this complex organism, are together the Body of Christ, or the Kingdom of Heaven.

Certain parts of the Body perform specific functions in God's Kingdom, aligned and interconnected with their own corresponding governmental functions (skin), and the many other parts with theirs, and so on. Governmental leaders do cover, in a sense, but not, for instance, as a lid covers. They are part of the rest of the Body, with the same life, the same blood, and the same overall Kingdom purposes. Only their functions are different.

The physical skin does not smother, rule over, nor in any way control the inner workings of the body. So it is with the spiritual skin, or governmental leaders and structures. All of the spiritual Body is cohesive and held together, interconnected, inseparable, and growing together in the Life of God. He is before all things, and by Him all things consist (Colossians 1:17).

GOVERNMENTAL ALIGNMENT AND PHYSICAL SKIN

Three weeks after our wedding, my husband, Richard, and I were involved in a major car accident. I was knocked unconscious, my husband stunned. The gasoline tank of our car exploded and fire licked at my skin until, in only a few precious moments, major damage had been done to what was, though I was totally unaware of it, the biggest organ of my body.

Richard dragged me out through the flames, and we were rushed in an ambulance to the emergency room and finally to the burn unit of a major hospital about thirty miles away. In our initial shock, we were thankfully unaware of the major trauma our bodies had suffered. But over the next months of physical agony, we learned in a most graphic way the vital importance of skin and what it means to us in everyday life. A battle began in an area of my body I had hardly been aware of up to this point in my life.

Amazing parallels can be drawn between the physical organ, skin, and those spiritual governmental "organs" provided for us by God. Wisdom and valuable applications can be derived from the inner workings of God's spiritual Body on earth, thus helping us to live a healthier Kingdom life, one of growth and prosperity. We will begin with some general observations.

- *The skin is the biggest organ of the body. It is an actual part of the body and it is also a protective covering for it at the same time.*

Various spiritual alignments make up a large part of the vital "organs" which then support the life of our spiritual Body. These relationships are part of who we are as we give and receive Kingdom strength one to another.

- *The skin is literally "knitted" to the body it serves and is a part of, so that it is difficult to tell where the skin ends and the body underneath begins.*

Unity is a mystery the Body of Christ has yet to grasp. Unity with the Lord should make His Presence such an integral part of our being that He is like the air that we breathe. Unity with the Lord's Body here on earth should mirror the same principle. This bond takes no thought of separation, independence, competition, jealousy or control.

Unfortunately, this kind of unity generally eludes us in our relationships on every level. When we, as a Body, begin to move in the direction of a John 17 dimension of love and unity, the impartation available through healthy governmental relationships will release great power which will strengthen and empower God's purposes in the earth.

> ...that they all may be one, as You, Father, are in Me, and I in You; that they also may be one in Us, that the world may believe that You sent Me. And the glory

which You gave Me I have given them, that they may be one just as We are one: I in them, and You in Me; that they may be made perfect in one, and that the world may know that You have sent Me, and have loved them as You have loved Me.

John 17:21-23 NKJV

- *The body is created to maintain and heal itself.*

Just as skin is constantly renewing itself and changing, governmental spiritual relationships do the same. They mature, grow, and make room for others to come forward in our daily lives. All of this happens in the normal course of living, without trauma and harm, and indeed with love and recognition of life's changing seasons.

- *Skin protects and holds in the life of the body while it carries out these functions of healing and maintenance.*

We are fearfully and wonderfully made (Psalm 139). As believers in Christ and new creatures made in His image, it is Christ in us Who is the hope of glory. In us resides resurrection power, healing virtue, and everything we need for healing and restoration. Healing and growth continues while we are learning this truth. Relationships provided by God help protect and hold us together while we grow and become whole and mature in Christ as the process of healing and growth continues.

- *When the skin is healthy, you hardly notice bumps, casual scrapes, and so many of the random encounters that everyday life brings.*

With healthy governmental relationships in place, "love hardly notices when it is done wrong" (1 Corinthians 13:5). Offenses and jabs shouldn't cause pain. The normal challenges of each day will not buffet and bruise, and we will know peace at the end of each day.

- *When damage has occurred however, the slightest invasion is a major source of pain. Exposed nerve endings, as in the case of skin damage, can be excruciatingly painful.*

Mind, will and emotions can actually function as nerve endings do, and can cause much pain. When proper spiritual alignments are not in place, this pain can be greatly magnified. Many times we are overly sensitive about misunderstandings, simply reacting to the overwrought emotions of others. The strength of Kingdom alignment brings healthy responses to these challenging situations, alleviating unnecessary pain and giving us the heavenly perspectives necessary to overcome life's traumas.

- *Skin doesn't continually shout its presence. It just exists, calmly and silently doing its job.*

Governmental relationships should be like the skin. If healthy and in place, they are barely noticed; however, if damaged or not functioning properly, they can bring pain, seeking attention. Proper relational coverings are not aggressive and assertive, drawing attention to themselves. They are like God; present, steadfast, immovable and at peace. Just as healthy skin does not inhibit the movement of the body, spiritual leadership, rather than control or restrict, should *facilitate* freedom of movement.

- *Skin can look fine, yet be seriously compromised in its job. A healthy outward appearance can be deceiving. Serious disease cannot always be identified simply by "looks."*

Often our relationships can look healthy on the surface, but actually be dysfunctional and harmful. Discernment and detection are needed in this as in all things pertaining to our spirit. Some governmental spiritual coverings are chosen for wrong reasons such as reputation, fame, or financial opportunities. The outer trappings of glitter and flash may not only hide a multitude of sins, but are no guarantee of the wisdom and love vital to the healthy protection of a true spiritual covering. On the other hand, persons in these important positions in our lives may not look or act as we would expect, but actually be extremely effective without being obvious.

- *Sometimes the skin must be cut to get to problems underneath, perhaps some kind of internal damage.*

God can deal with a problem directly by setting aside the covering temporarily and then knitting it back together just as skin is stitched back after surgery. Once I was asked to speak at a conference on the subject of "The Cutting Edge." The Lord revealed to me a definition: the cutting edge is the place where the sharp edge of the blade (the sword of the Word!) cuts the flesh (skin first!) and then the blood flows.

Sometimes a fresh perspective or a "specialist" is needed and brought in to deal with deeply entrenched problems. This can produce the effect of cut flesh and the pain of a wound. An established authority in our lives may have to step back temporarily to allow spiritual surgery, and even the covering itself may need adjustment or instruction. Humility can be a releasing anesthetic in these cases and healing can result from something as seemingly traumatic as surgery.

- *Scrape your skin off? One of the first things the body does is to provide a temporary cover while it rushes to heal the wound from underneath. The scab, or temporary cover, stays until the body grows new skin together under it.*

When an important alignment in our life is taken away unexpectedly, the grace of the Lord will come immediately to cover us until a proper and normal covering function is reestablished. How many of us, when in the midst of hurtful relationship trials, have been comforted by the soothing balm of the love of a friend, a pastor or a spouse? Sometimes a temporary pastor or organization can step in while painful transitional healing takes place.

- *Skin can be damaged, even severely, and the body can heal it from underneath; indeed it is meant to heal it from underneath, without the trauma of exposure!*

Has a situation or circumstance ever damaged your faith? In times of discouragement when the loss of faith, love or trust occurs, we must reach deep into God's heart. His Spirit inside of us can restore our soul and strengthen our inner man. Similarly, when problems are encountered with governmental persons in our lives, the Lord's way is to heal without the trauma and pain of complete exposure of the deep innermost parts of ourselves. In other words, He will heal without hurtful confrontations, accusations, harsh words, or abusive actions. Love will cover while wisdom heals.

All of us must learn to work out problematic relationships in the love of the Lord, healing and restoring one another even in the midst of conflicting opinions and ideas, without schism or "divorce." All too often we run. All too often we are forced to run. Both sides must provide the atmosphere of love, enabling us to remain steady.

"For whom the Lord loves He corrects, just as a father the son in whom he delights" (Proverbs 3:12, NKJV). The Lord delights in His children, and it is BECAUSE of that love that He chastens. The correction or discipline of the Lord can be meted out with such love that one hardly realizes he is being corrected. Holy Spirit comforts and heals, even in the midst of correction.

When we as human beings take matters into our own hands apart from the ways of the Lord, the soul reigns. Pride runs the show. Individuals in authority often have a need to be "right." The resulting trauma in one's life can take years to heal, causing suspicion of all authority, and an inability to submit and trust again.

THE BEAUTY OF KINGDOM ALIGNMENT

The beauty of governmental Kingdom alignment is like the beauty of the King Himself, ageless, and full of wonder. Like the seamless *harmonious unity* garment of the Lord, He has designed His Body to fit together in perfect harmony, the places they were first joined together now invisible in the light of such harmonious unity.

No one notices who leads or who follows, since the entire living mechanism operates together as smoothly and soundlessly as any well-designed "machine" should. This engine has no sand to grind the gears or mud to slow the wheels. This God-made vehicle operates in God-ordained principles, with no hitches, blips or halting in sight! God has joined it together! Let man acquiesce and leaders, ministries and followers shoulder together, joyous in God's harmony!

Just as the physical body cannot live without the protective covering of skin, in the Body of Christ, every person and every minister or organization needs the governmental spiritual accountability provided by the Lord.

This is true of leaders as well, no matter who they are, no matter how long they have been in ministry, how well known their name, how many churches they have started, schools they have attended, millions of dollars in the budget, souls they have saved or thousands who attend their meetings. EVERYONE needs proper alignment, protection, relationship and accountability as a responsible resident of the Kingdom of Heaven.

Let us rejoice in it! Let us accept it and hasten to obey it. For whom the Lord loves He both blesses and disciplines diligently. Let us embrace the perspectives of governmental alignment and make them a priority as we move into this new season.[3]

---

3   This chapter contains portions of the author's work, *The Importance of Covering*

SEVEN

Broken Alignment

Alignment in the Kingdom is about unity, an inseparable joining together of the eternal power of love and the purposes of the Life of God. In the beginning the earth was created to water itself (Genesis 2:6). So the divine network of the Kingdom functions in His grace and power, continuing to supply itself with strength in the midst of the battles and storms often accompanying the accomplishing of His purposes.

When networking established by our Father is broken, tearing and trauma, grief and pain can result from which it is often hard to recover. My experience with severe burns can be a graphic analogy of what can happen in these situations.

In the immediate care of burn injuries, dead skin must be stripped away before being replaced with grafted skin. Charred skin doesn't just naturally slough off or fall away. It stubbornly adheres to the body, even though dead and unable to function properly. When spiritual relationships are broken or stripped away, much of the same pain and trauma can result. The following examples are observable parallels which will help us to accurately navigate through challenging relationships.

- *Damaged or dead skin stays attached to the body and must be removed before other skin can be grafted. When skin is stripped away, agony is the result.*

In the case of damaged spiritual coverings or injured relationships, often the dynamics of the former relationship must be severed completely before new relationships can be put into place. Certainly healing and restoration should always be the goal, but there are times when relating in the former way becomes impossible. Quick recognition of this and the application of wise counsel make the pain of transition much less traumatic.

- *As the skin is removed, vital life-giving body fluids escape. They must continually be replaced; if they are not, the body dehydrates.*

Much time should be spent in His Presence and in His Word during transitional relationships. Our spirit must be strengthened during this critical time. Our reinforced spirit will give our soul the grace to overcome. Even as water is replenished in an overflowing fountain, the life of the Kingdom washes and continually refreshes and heals even as pain depletes our reservoir. His river never runs dry! When we feel we have lost our life-supply He is standing by, often through one of His servants, to pour in, pour in, pour in, until the dry and depleted place is once again a place of living water.

- *In initial burn care, the greatest danger is infection. When skin is compromised, the body is opened to germs and disease.*

When leadership relationships are damaged, poisonous thinking, hurtful words, and unwise actions can set off chain reactions of the same nature until an unnecessary war zone results. The grace and peace of the Lord carries us even as prayer supports and uplifts us in these challenging times.

Moral decay in leaders is often like the sources of infection to our physical body. Instead of the strength leadership is called to impart, they can open us to, even infect us, with their own illness or diseases. There is often a loss of anointing, perspective, and wisdom. Without accountability and submission to others in their own lives, many leaders fall into deception. Dangerous directions and choices can be the result. Disappointment and disillusionment in our leaders may cause irreparable damage to the Body of Christ.

Far too much pain is caused to innocent people when leaders choose not to submit to wise counsel. Who counsels leaders? Even in a temptation-yielding time of separation from God, wise counsel should be sought by the conflicted and extended graciously by other leaders with a true Father's anointing.

- *With the loss of skin, the look of the body is abnormal and frightening to the eyes. Nerve endings are exposed, greatly increasing sensitivity to every touch.*

In times of transition and/or painful restoration, things may look abnormal and even frightening. Discernment may be threatened, or we may see things we don't normally see. These are the times to keep our eyes on the Lord in His perfect peace, seeing the invisible and not the visible!

When we are adrift and alone without the comfort of wise counselors and mature leadership, we can be unusually sensitive to the darts of the wicked one. In these times, so many relationships are damaged or turbulent because of super-sensitivity to the words, tone, or actions of unsuspecting friends and co-workers. Feelings of rejection can begin to take hold and we become more vulnerable and open to additional injury.

The strength of the Lord and His Body protect us from unnecessary pain. What would one do without the shield of faith! Without the breastplate of righteousness! Without the wise counsel of a pastor or the prayers of others! Intercessors within the Body of Christ are like Emergency Response Teams, hastening to our rescue to head off the enemy who would prey on us in our times of weakness and pain. Pick up the phone! The ERT is only a ring away!

Turn to one of the Lord's servants. Refuse isolation. The Body was created to heal itself. Let one of the trusted minister to that exceptionally sensitive and painful wound. The healing touch of the Master's hand is most often felt through one of His unlikely, unrecognized, and unsuspected healers!

- *The body cannot live indefinitely without skin. Many injured too severely die because even grafting new skin is not an option.*

The Grace of the Lord covers us in transition. However, we cannot and must not live in transition forever. God's proper order and government must be in effect for a normal healthy spiritual life. Too often the walking wounded in the army of God are left to die on the battlefield, with no attempt to treat the wounds or apply a new covering for fresh protection. Most of us know those who have totally left their walk with the Lord because of wounds received that were never treated and healed.

No matter the pain leaders have caused you in the past, reach out to the Lord through another of His chosen ones. Don't reject everybody else simply because one disappointed, failed or injured you. Trust the Lord. He is the One who resurrected His Body, and He is the One who will continue that life-source, even in the midst of the agony of human life and death throes.

- *After every vestige of dead skin is removed, skin is taken from another part of the body and applied to the area. Sometimes an artificial graft is used until a permanent one can be applied.*

CHANGING LEADERSHIP ALIGNMENTS

The Lord may change governmental relationships, but they should not be detached without His gentle, loving and wise guidance. When the season of a former relationship is at an end, a new one must be put into that place. It could be that temporary or transitional oversight must be established until permanent leadership is available. This is a wise solution if much time is required to select a replacement. It is often ill-advised to rush into new relationships without proper development and necessary bonding.

Suspicion can often grow out of unhealed hurtful relationships from the past and can taint or harm healthy growth in new relationships. It is vital to forgive those from the past in order to move on to a productive future with new people in new places. New is not always bad, it can be better. Allow the Lord to make all things new!

Timing
Trust in His timing as He transitions past alliances and brings in new relationships and establishes new bases of operation. Unwise

removal of protective relationships ahead of God's timetable can cause great pain, and emotional scarring as well. Unfortunately, there are those who never recover from the wounds and will bear emotional and spiritual scars the rest of their lives.

Most of us tend to be impatient with God's timetable. We rush into, and out of, situations and relationships unwisely without giving due attention to God's timing. We base our decisions on our perceptions and how we feel instead of asking the question, what is God saying? What is His will in this matter? Leaving a church or a relationship should proceed exactly like entering it should be: at the direction and hand of the Lord, and *in His timing*.

Allow God's timetable, indelibly linked to His healing, restorative nature, to operate the signature moves in our lives. Because God does not live in a time-space dimension, the laser of His Light strikes accurately across the darkness of our confusion into our realm of time, more accurately than *His light strikes* human nature ever could. He knows, and He *accurately* will move. Wait for it. You will heal and be at peace while you wait.

Removing or leaving governmental relationships should be gentle, loving, and blessed, much like a revolving door: smooth and painless. The graciousness of genteel courtesy so reflects the kindness of the King that we part leaving grace and blessings behind, and we come together in His love, expecting and resting in God alone.

DEVELOPING RELATIONSHIPS

On occasion new connections or beginning relationships may be seen through a golden haze which can only be known as the "honeymoon" stage. We become impressed with our new authorities and spiritual gifts or with what the Lord is developing through them. But as relationships develop and the romance of the honeymoon phase transitions into a true knowledge of these "clay vessels," criticism and dissatisfaction may begin to creep in. Once the honeymoon is over, what then?

At all times, there must be awareness that no one is perfect. There is no perfect church, no perfect pastor, no perfect minister, and no perfect spouse. We have all fallen short of the glory of God, and we are all earthen vessels with our physical bodies still firmly planted on terra firma. Learning the shortcomings and weaknesses of one another on any level must produce compassion and love, not judgment and criticism. Most of the time when we are in that latter mode, we are so focused on the problems of others that our own never surface in our minds.

We expect perfection from those we admire. We, however, are the ones who put them up on pedestals to begin with. The star mentality must give way to the issues of the heart, those that most concern God. Fame, wealth, and power are dangerous attributes for God's people to experience. Better obscurity or persecution than to fall from the pedestals of the world's fickle opinions.

Ministers must not only admit, but *glory* in their weaknesses, that His strength might be perfected (2 Corinthians 12:9). Admittedly, this is a hard concept to grasp. Few are willing to recognize, in fact many will not confess to weaknesses and failures. The spotlight of the public eye can do strange things to a person's character. The public wants their leaders to be perfect, so leadership sometimes convinces themselves that they are. This results in consciences encased in calluses and hard shells.

changes with grace, color and style

But if God's chosen, in humility, confess their faults, they free those who would try to exalt leadership beyond God's perfect design. Out of this humility, anyone called into oversight ministries for others can have much greater strength and wisdom, because it will be His nature and character, and not their own.

As new relationships evolve, they must not be expected nor even desired to be similar to the former. Let God do a new thing! He always takes us to new levels and greater victories. Let go of the past and revel in the provision of the Lord.

New relationships need time to develop and strengthen. We must slowly and carefully move into new and demanding involvements and commitments. We must learn to trust and accept new relationships, allowing for differences in temperament, personality, perceptions, and ways of operation. This will take time. Allow the patience of the Lord to keep your heart.

Healing of Wounds

I have recovered from the wounds and scars of the trauma of burns in my life. God has healed me, both inside and out. There are still scars visible, but they are no longer painful. That season has changed and I am better and stronger for the rich lessons and wisdom learned through suffering. As with the healing of governmental relationships, now I can look forward to what the Lord has in store for the next seasons, knowing that His will for me is *enlightening* perfect. It is so freeing to allow the seasons to *hope* change with grace, color, and style.

CHANGING SEASONS

Often in the case of governmental relationships, the Lord will bring one season to a natural close before moving us on to the next assignment. He determines the time. It does not have to be painful. We can hear His voice and follow His direction on both sides of the relationship. The grace and peace of the Lord allow us to transition with joy, unhampered by hurt, offense, unforgiveness, or other unnecessary negative emotions.

In nature, changing seasons can be extraordinarily beautiful. When summer turns toward fall, refreshing cool winds blow across blistered landscapes. Startling color marks fall's march to winter. Tender green shoots, nesting birds, and brilliant flowers herald the coming of spring. Lush vegetation and fragrant winds usher in the warmth of summer.

Can we learn nature's acceptance of changing seasons? Can we view transition with joy, trusting that the Lord is ordering our steps and making everything work for our good? Transition times in relationships and in churches can be full of peace. Our perspective must be full of trust, peace, and expectation of the Lord's goodness and plan for our lives.

My husband, Richard, is a morning person. I am not. One of several problems that I have in the mornings is that I have extremely low blood pressure. So when I wake up in the morning, I experience feelings similar to those of awakening from a general anesthesia. I am not pleased when morning arrives. Consciousness returns slowly but my body does not want to move.

Once, on a rare morning when awareness of the day actually came to me before Richard woke up, I lay listening to him snore. Suddenly, one second after his last snore, he said loudly,

"What are you going to do today?"

I groaned. The bane of my existence, Richard's hyperactive mornings. Finally I questioned him.

"Why do you like mornings so much?"

After a thoughtful silence he replied, "It's a time of great expectation."

"Expectation of what?" I asked.

And he answered, "Of everything."

This is a profound truth for those of us who know the Lord. When night recedes into the glorious transition of sunrise, what should be our perspective? Great expectation! Because God has plans for us: hope, and a great future. He declares this in Jeremiah 29:11-12: "For I know the plans I have for you," declares the Lord, "plans to prosper you and not to harm you, plans to give you hope and a future." (NIV)

The light of the righteous grows brighter and brighter until the full day. Pray for the enlightening hope of expectation. God is good, especially in transition. Because in Him, transition means that change is upon us and the old we are so weary of is on the way out. The old day has died, and a new and gorgeous sun is rising to light new terrain and new vistas. Dawn is the transition of darkness into light. Rejoice when the day dies because a new dawn and a new day will make all things new!

One constant upon which we can depend is this: the devil has a plan for our lives and his plan is to skin us alive and to strip us of every vestige of life. His plan is to break us in every place of health and strength. But don't despair! More constant and dependable than any plan of the enemy is that our God has an eternal plan for us. His purpose, which stands forever, is to protect, heal, and restore.

As we seek the face of the Lord and His wisdom in Kingdom direction, we must pursue every avenue that aligns us with His plan for us. We trust that He takes the broken and makes it whole and new, and we rejoice in the future ahead of us, secure in His hand.

Let us line up with the principles of the Word! Let us line up with the networking of the Body of Christ and the purposes of the Lord! God give us the revelation that governmental relationships are a vital, life-giving priority in our lives! [4]

---

4   This chapter contains portions of the author's work, *The Importance of Covering*

EIGHT

Kingdom Government: Use and Misuse

Ordained and gifted by God to carry out His assignments, leaders may be in the right place at the right time and still, because of human nature, improperly apply the authority given to them. Leaders often grow stressed and beleaguered with too many responsibilities, thus reducing their effectiveness. Some become corrupted by money, fame and/or power. Others may simply be uninformed or immature. But whatever the cause, the result in the Kingdom can be mild to catastrophic. We all know people who were so wounded by mistakes in leadership that they have never recovered.

The condition of the leadership itself should bear much scrutiny as we consider relational government in times of trauma and challenging circumstances. When important changes are being made governmentally and all concerned are undergoing difficulties, great care must be exercised in the interaction between all parties.

Often we forget that God's leaders and generals are still human beings themselves, as they carry out this earth-walk in frail and flawed clay pots. When unwise decisions and actions proceed from oversight ministries, there must be checks and balances in place for the well-being of all.

Wise alignment and accountability within Kingdom government will allow grace, healing and adjustments to be made when motives begin to veer off course, leaving the pure wisdom from above behind.

MOTIVES WITHIN GOVERNMENTAL ALIGNMENT

Misuse of Authority

The authority of God can never be separated or isolated from His gentle, kind, and humble nature. Human beings, however, sometimes wield what they believe to be the authority of God with such unwise application that it cannot and should not be tolerated. The intent behind the authority and action is vitally important, particularly if there is already existing damage or serious problems that need addressing.

Leadership applied wrongly can cause a great waste of emotional energy and precious time. Sadly, these mistaken intentions have caused many believers to leave an active church life and the Lord's service completely. But when they stop and listen for His voice, He will lead with peace and guide His called into the fruitful pastures of rest.

Kingdom alliances should be chosen wisely, making certain that it is God's "match" so that there is unity within the connection. God's union will grow stronger and more natural day by day. But many times becoming a leader who oversees others is an excuse for independent thinking and power. The question one must ask is: Who oversees the overseer? If the pastor, apostle, or leader uses that

wise Kingdom alliances

place of authority as an excuse for lack of accountability themselves, then all who are aligned together with him will be affected by incorrect perspectives and methods.

It is damaging when a leader uses the Lord's authority to curb a believer's freedom or violate the respect of his calling. The Lord's way is for each person to come to Him freely, developing his own gifts and relationship with Him. Every person who follows God should listen for and recognize His voice for himself, and then obey using his own discernment. Governmental Kingdom alignment is meant to prepare the way for this freedom, not to usurp it.

In what is now thought of as the "shepherding" movement, man, in an attempt to implement God's truth, added some of his own nature and opinions to the mix. In many instances, the additional control resulted in situations where a leader as "overseer" interfered and controlled intimate details and decisions in the lives of individuals and families within his or her care. In 1 Peter, the Lord gives serious warnings about constraint and dictatorial leadership by leaders of His flock.

I warn and counsel the elders among you (the pastors and spiritual guides of the church) ...Tend (nurture, guard, guide, and fold) the flock of God that is [your responsibility], not by coercion or constraint, but willingly; not dishonorably motivated by the advantages and profits [belonging to the office], but eagerly and cheerfully; not domineering [as arrogant, dictatorial, and overbearing persons] over those in your charge, but being examples (patterns and models of Christian living) to the flock (the congregation).

1 Peter 5:1-3, AMP

Domineering or overbearing leadership will result in immaturity, and can quench fledgling gifts and developing ministries. This dominance may also begin to foster despair and apathy. Ephesians 4 clearly instructs us that the apostle, prophet, pastor, evangelist and teacher are given by God to equip and raise up His people not only to mature them, but to be *like Him.*

The King of our Kingdom leads through His generals and tenderly guides through His chosen shepherds. God's chosen headship will care for those belonging to the King, and treat them accordingly. Leadership is chosen and appointed to raise and lift up, to build and equip, and to continue to perfect all that concerns the ones in their charge.

... His intention was the perfecting and the full equipping of the saints (His consecrated people), that they should do the work of ministering toward building up Christ's body (the church), that it might develop until we all attain oneness in the faith and in the comprehension of the full and accurate knowledge of the Son of God, that we might arrive at **really mature manhood** (the completeness of personality which is nothing less than the standard height of Christ's own perfection), the measure of the stature of the fullness of the Christ and the completeness found in Him.

Ephesians 4:12-13, AMP

In this powerful scripture, reaching "mature manhood" depends on "oneness in the faith and full and accurate knowledge of the Son of God." With this being the ultimate goal, it should be clear that the path is not through overbearing and controlling styles of leadership.

Control

In the church today, there is widespread misunderstanding of the principle of oversight. This confusion is the reason the word "covering" is such a sensitive word. The concept of covering should not mean that one person is *under* and another is *over*. *God* is our covering. We are aligned to Him. He is in us and we in Him.

It is the desire to be *over* which has fostered much of the resistance in those who oppose the covering principle. Man seems to have a need to be over in wielding authority, and sheep to believe leaders when they insist that they should be under. Unfortunately, this tends to be about dominance and control on the part of the leader. The star mentality of exalting one over the masses fits in all too easily with the dominate/ subjugate leanings in some covering ministries.

Overbearing leadership results in dependency on others. It occurs in churches and relational networks when control and manipulation masquerade in the name of love and care, or in the "giving of the word of the Lord." This will make the individual less accountable and responsible to God, while being more accountable to a human being who is standing in the position as a leader thought to be led by the Lord. What the Lord is saying to us directly diminishes, and it is believed that we must hear through our chosen deliverer. Courage to make choices and decisions that should be a part of the normal course of healthy spiritual growth is then lost.

In rightly relating Kingdom governmental relationships, God flows through His Body to cover or protect, to equip, and to strengthen. For example, apostles are vessels in whom the apostolic grace of God flows out to minister the Christ Gift, or Grace, of the Apostle. There is only God-given authority and oversight. There is governmental order. There should not be domination or subjugation. There are no officials, rulers, or kings in God's Kingdom. In His Kingdom there is one Official and one Ruler. There is one King, and He is God!

We are called to stand! We are called to charge forward! We are called to fly! Kingdom leadership will lend us wings and provide the waiting eagle's updraft, enabling him to fly. Kingdom leadership will aid us as we sniff the wind and prepare to rise to new heights. True Kingdom oversight will encourage and give us freedom to fly, and then rejoice in our journey.

Kingdom leadership lends us wings

TRUE KINGDOM OVERSIGHT

True Godly leadership in the Kingdom should function from the Father's perspective. Leaders are admonished to lead and guide gently as the Great Shepherd does. God's leaders are not meant to be coaches, running team plays, correcting and criticizing while pushing after other goals, some not necessarily God's. A leader's function is to *serve*, not to rule! Jesus Himself said He came not to be served but to serve. True oversight in humility will release peace, and encourage the fulfillment of dreams.

> And we urge you, brethren, to recognize those who labor among you, and are over you in the Lord and admonish you, and to esteem them very highly in love for their work's sake. Be at peace among yourselves.
> 1 Thessalonians 5:12-13, NKJV

In this scripture regarding oversight, the word for 'admonish' means to caution or reprove gently. As we study the Lord's leadership principles, it is discovered that gentleness, kindness, and love run like refreshing clear water, with the bubbling of joy alongside. The apostle Paul often began his admonitions to those in his charge with the salutations, Grace and Peace to you! We, the sheep, likewise are encouraged to obedience and submission. Christ's leaders will give an account to the Lord for their care of the sheep, and the sheep are to receive their shepherd's service with gladness and joy.

We all, leaders and followers together, must lay down our need to be right. We must surrender the need for admiration, adulation, affirmation, and for power and dominance. Many problems today in the Body of Christ will be eliminated as leaders operate in humility and wisdom. There will be peace in the midst of any storm, and the people of God will have the safe havens and places of refuge He intended among His Body.

In all things pertaining to service in and for the Lord, both leaders and followers must remember that their labor, time, energy, and love, is unto the Lord. "Whatever you do, work at it with all your heart, as though you were working for the Lord and not for men. Remember that the Lord will give you as a reward what he has kept for His people. For Christ is the real Master you serve" (Colossians 3:22-25 TEV). He is the King! And as we serve one another, we wash His feet and dry them with our hair.

SERVANTS IN THE KINGDOM

Jesus said, I come not to be served, but to serve. This Lord of the Ages demonstrated this statement when, girded with a towel, He washed the dusty and probably smelly feet of His disciples. And thus He demonstrated a profound and piercing principle of Life in the Kingdom. The greatest will be the servant of all. The highest will bow low, and the ruler of all will humbly lend his hand to the dirtiest, least desired task.

This King of the Highest came to a beleaguered, embattled, embittered earth, and laying His glory in the dust, lent His splendor to the weak, the confused, and to the unresponsive masses. He was not threatened by ignorance or skepticism, or even outright belligerence. He had come to serve, and serve He did, giving His life to insure that humanity might see and understand the true nature of a lay-your-life-down Servant Leader King.

Sadly, in today's world, there are leaders who assume that because they have "poured into" the sheep, that the sheep "owe" them loyalty, service, and even lifelong commitment. Certainly loyalty and servanthood apply in relationships, but the axiom, "I have given to you, therefore you owe me" is not a Godly principle. Leaders in God's Kingdom serve the sheep because it is their mandate from God and their joy. What the sheep do or do not do in return is out of the leaders' control and should be out of their expectations.

Jesus gave with no thought of return. So must we. He poured

out His life daily, not counting the cost or the hours. So must we. He lived and died, serving His Father despite suffering rejection, hatred, and scorn. So must we. He walked the dusty roads seeking out the lost, frightened, and persecuted. And when finding them, He stopped and gave more and more of His time and life. So must we. To be true servants in the Kingdom, we must lay down our lives without thought, without prejudice, without prior knowledge, and without impatience, following every need to provide what is required, just as Jesus did and still does today, a Servant of the Kingdom.

BOUNDARIES

When pondering boundaries, one remembers the man with the appearance of bronze and a measuring rod in His hand (Ezekiel 40:3). Observed by the prophet, he measured and defined the dwelling places of God. After the subsequent encounter with the God of glory, mysterious and profound thought was poured out to the people of the King, and God's rule continued to expand itself. Boundaries can and should exist to expand and define the dominion of the King, and thus the security and well-being of His people.

One of the biggest pitfalls in accepting or submitting to the idea of relational or governmental oversight in the Kingdom of God is that the requirements and expectations are the same for everyone. Our challenge is that in our minds we have our own ideas of what those requirements should be. Practically speaking, what should the requirements and definitions of governmental Kingdom alignment be? Where are the boundaries and how do we expect them to apply to our lives? Can we, like the man in linen, measure them with God's measuring line?

Often the reason relationships don't work for us is because we try to build them according to our own understanding. The truth is that what we want and what God knows we need are often different, and we don't always have the understanding to discern the difference. We must come to a place where we release our own ideas and opinions and let go of the boxes and structures we have carefully built with our intellect, desire and ambition.

As we relax our opinions and perspectives, we begin to realize that God provides abundantly more than we can ask, however, not always in the way we expect. This applies when we look at the practicality of governing relationships, and all the complexities involved.

Many of us have several governmental organizations and ministries in our lives; each may serve a different purpose in our oversight. In many instances there may be overlapping of these purposes. One ministry may have several different functions. The point to remember is that there are differences in ability according to circumstances, geographical positioning, experience and calling. Therefore we must let *God* design the blueprint and define and employ the boundaries for the structural relationships in our lives.

CHOOSING OUR PLACES OF ALIGNMENT

Although it may sound harsh, in life we either make a choice, or it is made for us. The choices made for us are not usually as pleasing to us as the ones we choose for ourselves. It is essential for us to have God as our Guide, ordering our steps and establishing our boundaries. Our choices may not always be wise, but choosing *God's* choice is. We as God's people enjoy utilizing the freedom of will that He gave to us. Using that will to follow His is the greatest of all wisdom. We all fit into the Kingdom, and have our places of alignment in God's plan.

Rightly positioned, we will shine and His power will accomplish His will through us. Rightly connected in the electrical power grid of the Kingdom, the lightnings of the electrical current of God will flash through us and the people around us, as we draw on and transmit Kingdom power one to another.

Humility

When we choose particular relationships in our lives, it is important that those we give the right to speak into our lives move in God's love, His grace, and, most importantly, His humility. Jesus placed great emphasis on people with no guile. Authorities who have input into our lives should be ones who themselves move in submission. Pride puts up a smoke screen, limiting clear vision, and endangering all those around.

Clothe (apron) yourselves, all of you, with humility [as the garb of a servant, so that its covering cannot possibly be stripped from you, with freedom from pride and arrogance] toward one another. For God sets Himself against the proud (the insolent, the overbearing, the disdainful, the presumptuous, the boastful)--[and He opposes, frustrates, and defeats them], but gives grace (favor, blessing) to the humble.

Therefore humble yourselves [demote, lower yourselves in your own estimation] under the mighty hand of God, that in due time He may exalt you...

1 Peter 5:5-6, AMP

Humility is that low, sweet root, from which all other virtues grow. Humility will beguile pride, and woo the disdainful. Humility will cause the idols to topple, and murmuring deceptions to be quieted. Humility is the unexpected source of power, authority incognito, that can cause even the highest walls to tumble.

Humility will gentle the wildest heart and the most frightened and skeptical gaze. Humility loves; pride pushes away. Humility reaches out no matter the resistance, and abides quietly through raging storms. Humility, judging self unworthy, will rule justly and non-judgmentally, while pride lords over all. Humility cries out without voice to trumpet trust and lays its glory in the dust of the needs of others.

Humility hides, but accomplishes what armies could not. Humility wins the battle without trying, striving, and without even suiting up the armor. For humility comes not to battle, but to rest from the battle.

humility comes to rest from battle

Humility will disarm the toughest weapon, and remove the desire to fight from the mightiest warrior. This is what we should seek, not riches, fame or power. We should seek humility, for then we will be like the King.

Life

God's direction to the children of Israel was to choose life; His admonition is to choose blessing, not cursing. The fruit of any Godly relationship should be life and blessing. If places of alignment produce depression, frustration, irritation, or bitterness, it is time to re-evaluate the situation and seek the Lord's wisdom concerning a change. The Life of the Kingdom will flow unhindered and uninhibited through true Kingdom leadership, just as the life of the vine flows into the branches, giving strength to grow, change and become.

> For with You is the fountain of life; in Your light we see light.
> Psalm 36:9, NKJV

Wisdom

Proverbs is very clear about the value of wisdom. At the direction of the Lord, we will search for those who have input into our lives from among the wise. We seek those with more wisdom than we have, more love, more experience, and more Godly authority. We seek those who are closer to the Lord than ourselves, and who walk in great humility. We know the spirit by the fruit it produces.

We should ask ourselves, What is the fruit of the ministry with which we are contemplating alignment, and what is the condition of the people within its sphere of influence? Solomon asked for wisdom. What is the leadership in this ministry requesting from God?

> The fear of the LORD is the beginning of wisdom, and
> the knowledge of the Holy One is understanding.
> Proverbs 9:10, NKJV

Those who hunger and thirst after wisdom and after the knowledge of God will foster great depth in those around them. They will see and drink of the fruits of this close and personal walk with the Holy One.

Honor

Sadly, honor is a quality which sometimes seems difficult to find in the Body of Christ today. Yet it is a command of the Lord. Be kindly affectioned one to another with brotherly love; in honor preferring one another (Romans 12:10, KJV).

What is honor? In this scripture the word honor means value, esteem, or dignity. Yet so often we dishonor one another. Leaders dishonor by looking condescendingly down on those in their charge. Sheep dishonor by being rebellious, critical, and judgmental—

characteristics far removed from the attributes of God.

A dictionary definition of honor is "to revere, to respect, to treat with deference and submission; to treat with due civility and respect in the ordinary intercourse of life." If we are to be like God in our relationships, we must honor, serve and prefer one another.

> What is man that thou art mindful of him? And the son of man, that thou visitest him? For thou hast made him a little lower than the angels, and hast crowned him with glory and honor.
>
> Psalm 8:4-5, KJV

In this scriptural passage, the Lord likens honor to a crown. No one knows the imperfect heart of man as the Lord does, yet He still chooses to cover the heads of His chosen with crowns of glory and honor. Now is the time for demonstrating honor to one another, whether deserved or not. Kindness, honor, and grace are the hallmarks of alignment in the Kingdom of God and should be exercised by His chosen.

As the world views the Kingdom, O God, let them see the representatives of the Kingdom demonstrating honor and serving one another, speaking of each other with gentle grace, loving favor, and the oil of honor. Let the world be drawn to His leaders because of the honor shown between them. Let the Kingdom be another world, clean of the one they are accustomed to; clean of dishonor, disrespect, and scorn. Honor will displace the hard calluses of the world's ways with the purity of trust that honor brings. Let the crown of honor shine into the darkness of the world's suspicion and bring visions of the King, to whom all honor, glory and power be forever and ever, amen.

Anointing

The world needs the oil of the Holy Spirit. It needs the anointing of a gusher. The Body of Christ requires the power of God. We as leaders must allow the deep workings, the drillings of the Lord, in our lives to hit that mother lode. We are in a time when a change must come in the degree of the power of the Lord which we release as we minister in His name. It is time for the oil not to have to be pumped and pumped and pumped. We are ready for a GUSHER: not a little drip, but the thousand-barrels-a-day kind.

The anointing breaks the yoke and every one of us has that anointing within us. Many, even those in leadership, just don't know how to release it or let it out. That is what God is teaching us in this hour by the revelation of His Spirit. As He digs and drills deep into our being, He opens the fountains of the deep and calls them forth out of our midst (Genesis 7:11).

The rivers of anointing are simply awaiting release. The great barriers and dams set by the enemy are about to come crashing down, and the pent-up powerhouses of anointing within God's chosen are about to come rushing, pouring, and gushing out upon the desperate. Let us align ourselves and the ones we love with those who flow and drip and glisten with the powerful, life-changing, disease-healing, devil-defying anointing of the great Holy Spirit.

rushing, pouring, and gushing

> And it shall come to pass in that day, that his burden shall be taken away from off thy shoulder, and his yoke from off thy neck, and the yoke shall be destroyed because of the anointing.
>
> Isaiah 10:27, KJV

Advocate and Mediator

Once, in a conversation with a pastor friend, we began discussing a situation in his church. One of his sheep was a frequent problem, even to other ministries. I was so impressed with his gentle love and wisdom as he explained his counsel to this person, and firmly stated that he would not ask the person to leave his church. "I am his pastor," he said. His commitment was clear. Helping his sheep to change and grow is his calling, regardless of their present stage of growth or immaturity.

Jesus is our Advocate, Judge and Mediator. He is *for* us, and if God be for us, who can be against us? Governmental ministries in our lives must be our advocates, our mediators, and our intercessors. These attributes are the ultimate examples of unconditional love. Jesus is the Repairer of the Breach. Can we be no less? He is Wonderful, our Counselor, and our Prince of Peace. Is this what is being released as oversight ministries into the Kingdom? Is this what the Body of Christ receives as those who are seeking relational oversight in the Body of Christ?

None are capable of the perfection of our Lord. With the arm of flesh, there is no ability to govern with the grace and consistent love of Jesus. It is His strength, His love, and His power. It is His Kingdom, and His leaders, in proper Kingdom alignment, that will bring His protection, strength, and encouragement to His Body.

The Sustaining Power of the Lord

> Cast your burden on the LORD, and He shall sustain you;
> Psalm 55:22, NKJV

The stress and strain of leadership will rest upon His shoulders as leaders rest and lay their burdens on Him (Isaiah 9:6). Yes, the overwhelming burdens laid on leaders can be rolled onto the Lord. Then His sustaining power carries, motivates, and energizes.

Misuse in Kingdom government often results from weariness and apathy. But the Lord is the Shepherd of all! When God's leaders allow the great Shepherd and pastor of our souls to comfort, heal and restore in the midst of battle, they can pick up the banner of the Cross once again with confidence, boldness and courage for the next battle and the next victory. Our Lord leads us on to victory! He will shoulder our burdens and sustain us.

The Lord is taking Kingdom government to a new level. He is removing, changing, refreshing, restoring, and giving revelation in this time of great expectation. How wonderful to realize that things as we have known them are being traded in for the new improved models, the heavenly designs intended from the beginning. It is time to take a deep breath, relax, and watch God as He causes leadership and government as we know it to be reborn, knowing that this process is the next step in bringing us closer to divine order and heavenly Life.[5]

---

5   This chapter contains portions of the author's work, *The Importance of Covering*

Kingdom Alignment

NINE

Financial Alignment : The Riches of the Kingdom

Have you ever stood at the window on one of those dark and windless days when the rain comes down everywhere as though it has been poured out of some vast, eternal bucket? It falls in such an unmeasured, relentless flow that it thunders into the earth and you wonder where it can all go, and surely the heavens will run dry of it soon. But the skies never seem to tire of releasing their endless burden, and soon you tire first and then retire to a book or a nice cheery fire.

Or have you sat on a huge boulder at the foot of an immense waterfall, near enough to feel occasional spray, gazing at the towering column of raging water and wondering what dry place has been left once all those tons of water have deserted it for more favored climes? Or in the midst of a hurricane, have you watched angry tidal waves batter the coast with frightening power so out of control of all of man's extensive and clever scientific wonders?

Even in nature, we see the display of God's power and the immensity of His vast ability, and yes, even His willingness and desire, to POUR OUT of His boundless supply and His unlimited power, His unqualified and lavish goodness, joy, exuberance, and love. How can we align ourselves with the amazing nature of the King and ruler of our realm?

> The heavens declare the glory of God; and the
> firmament shows His handiwork. Day unto day utters
> speech, and night to night reveals knowledge. There is
> no speech nor language where their voice is not heard.
> Their line [sound] has gone out through all the earth,
> and their words to the end of the world.
>
> Psalm 19:1-4a, NKJV

ALIGNING WITH THE PRINCIPLE OF POURING OUT

Throughout scripture, as well as the earth in which we live, the character of God is revealed in an unmeasured, unprecedented flow of the giving of life. God is the giver of all good and perfect gifts, and He is the giver of life. We see an example of His uncalculated pouring as He opens the windows of heaven and pours out blessings far beyond the capacity to receive (Malachi 3:10). Our God can do exceedingly abundantly above all that we can ask or think. As we come to know Him, we realize that God does not HAVE love, He IS love. He does not HAVE light, He IS light. And so, He does not simply GIVE, He IS giving. And His giving is the constant out-flowing, freely pouring essence of all that He is. Through the windows of heaven, He pours a different quality of transforming life into another realm.

constant out-flowing

> For as the rain and the snow come down from heaven,
> and do not return there without watering the earth, and
> making it bear and sprout, and furnishing seed to the
> sower and bread to the eater; so shall My word be
> which goes forth from My mouth; it shall not return to
> Me empty, without accomplishing what I desire, and
> without succeeding in the matter for which I sent it.
>
> Isaiah 55:10-11, NASU

What a precious promise this is! To know that the Word of God which established the earth and every living thing still falls into our living earth, the new earth, the Body of Christ, and will not die there, but will accomplish the purposes of the Most High God. He perfects those things which concern us, and in a constant all-encompassing flow of divine life. His Word pours through earthen vessels in just as uncompromisingly powerful a flow as the thunder of rain in those longed-for latter rains before Harvest. "For He whom God has sent speaks the words of God; for He gives the Spirit without measure" (John 3:34).

Pouring Without Measure

In Jesus dwells the fullness of the Godhead bodily (Colossians 2:9). There is no limit to the measure of God in which He operates. But what is God's measure to man? We know that there has been given to every man the measure of faith (Romans 12:3). Would God give His Spirit in unlimited measure to Jesus and then give only limited measure to man? May it never be! For it is written,

> And He Himself gave some to be apostles, some prophets, some evangelists, and some pastors and teachers for the equipping of the saints for the work of ministry, for the edifying of the body of Christ, till we all come to the unity of the faith and of the knowledge of the Son of God, to a perfect man, to the measure of the stature of the fullness of Christ.
>
> Ephesians 4:11-13, NKJV

When a seed is planted, great care is taken to place it in a hole or container the right size for it. But in no way does the size of the seed or the place made for it limit the capacity of the plant to reach the height of maturity ordained for it. The container simply continues to enlarge to accommodate the growth. The tiny mustard seed bursts out of the earth into another realm, reaching to the skies in stately majesty. And so we, given a measure of faith, continue to water, weed, and fertilize, until from glory to glory we are come to the measure of the stature of the fullness of Christ-- in whom there is no limitation.

Pouring to Fullness

In like manner, in Kingdom financial realms, we give and pour and water, until fullness, not just prosperity as we know it, but the fullness of God is manifested and His nature and character rightly established in the area of need.

The Greek word for "fullness" in Ephesians 4:13 is "pleroma," meaning a full number, or full measure, suggesting that which has been completed. The word brings to mind a ship with a full cargo and crew. Fullness and completion: we are complete in Him! In Him, we experience the power of the fullness of eternity, of the force of the river whose streams make glad the city of God. The financial holes and needs in the Kingdom are complete in Him!

Today God's principle of pouring out is becoming more and more apparent as the Kingdom, the Body of Christ, learns to give. Many sermons have been taught and expounded upon over the last decades concerning the principle of giving in God's Word. Seed faith is sowing a seed into the need or the ministry of someone else. We have heard much about giving to get, or giving in order to receive blessing.

But as we apply ourselves to learn the principle of God's giving, we see that there is no thought of giving that there might be a return. It is simply an unmeasured, extraordinary pouring out, pouring out, pouring out. It is GOD'S principle of pouring out. In this pouring out He establishes a life-flow. He pours out and the earth answers by pouring back to Him, and as the earth answers by pouring back to Him, He pours out.

We see this when rain is loosed upon the earth. Then mist rises from the ground and seeds the clouds with moisture, whereby subsequent rain is released upon the obedient earth in glad showers. The cycle of life is begun all over again. The earth graphically illustrates the principle of God's nature as He pours out.

> And it will come about after this that I will pour out My Spirit on all mankind; and your sons and daughters will prophesy, your old men will dream dreams, your young men will see visions. And even on the male and female servants I will pour out My Spirit in those days.
> Joel 2:28-29, NASU

The pouring out of His Spirit upon His earth here is immediately followed by their pouring out of His Spirit in prophecy, dreams, and visions. The filled vessel is immediately and gladly pouring out that precious supply, knowing that the Source is never dry. Those of the Kingdom have learned His principle of measure: there is none. Man carefully measures after assiduously assessing the supply. Man therefore in measured pouring has a measured supply and consequently a measured return. Often man even decides the supply is too low to disturb. Let us wait until we build up a back log before we disturb the balance. No rain equals no growth and no growth equals death. When man carefully measures, he is choosing a way which seems right to him, but the end thereof is death (Proverbs 14:12).

"For in the way you judge, you will be judged; and by your standard of measure, it will be measured to you" (Matthew 7:2). Calculated measure contains an element of holding back. It is an attitude which calculates and decides "there is x amount in supply, x amount needed, and x amount allotted to fill that need, taking into account the price of pouring out." In essence it is a stingy spirit, taking more thought for self in lack of faith than acknowledging and operating in the flow of God's unprecedented, pouring out love.

As Jesus came upon the earth, a visible manifestation of all that God is, He poured out His life, His power, His Spirit, His character, His nature, and all the fullness of God, without measure into the seed and into the earth which God had given Him (John 17:2,8,22). God continues to pour out through His Son. The Spirit of Christ Jesus cried out in David's messianic prophecy, "I am poured out like water..." (Psalm 22:14).

King David was a forerunner of that second Adam Who thirsted upon the cross. While fleeing for his life into the caves and the rocks and the hills, David became very thirsty (2 Samuel 23:15). And so his mighty men went to draw, at the risk of their lives, from the wells of Bethlehem that he might have water. But David poured out this offering upon the ground; he poured out this precious substance brought at such a price upon the earth as an offering to the Lord.

David didn't save back enough to assuage his thirst and then empty the rest on the ground. He didn't tithe the water. He poured it out unreservedly before the Lord of Glory. Even so Jesus poured out His life upon and into the earth as an offering to His Father. And He has bought us that we might pour out into the earth our lives and the preciousness of all our substance, even as Jesus our elder brother poured out, that life might come. This is the great reciprocity of God.

When God gave His Son, it pleased Him to bruise Him, because Jesus justified many, pouring out His soul unto death (Isaiah 53:10-12). There was no stinting in the outpouring of life to save many lives. There is no measure in God's mercy. "Thy lovingkindness, O Lord, extends to the heavens, Thy faithfulness reaches to the skies" (Psalm 36:5). There is no measure in the love of God, so majestically described in the old hymn,

> O the deep, deep love of Jesus,
> Vast unmeasured, boundless, free!
> Rolling as a mighty ocean in its fullness over me!
> Underneath me, all around me,
> Is the current of Thy love--
> Leading onward, leading homeward,
> To Thy glorious rest above!

"Then shall we know, if we follow on to know the Lord: His going forth is prepared as the morning; and He shall come unto us as the rain, as the latter and former rain unto the earth" (Hosea 6:3, KJV). The torrential floods of the latter rains have scarcely begun to thunder upon our earth.

There is coming such a flood of His grace, His love, and His manifested power, that surely all the fountains of the deep have been loosed, and the windows of heaven opened. We shall never come to the end of our God, and His infinite love and yearning, brooding and hovering over this, His garden and His beloved.

ALIGNING WITH GOD'S PRINCIPLE
OF GROWTH AND INCREASE

As God set the worlds into motion, His principle of multiplication was also set into motion. His dream was not to create a one-time permanent object which would remain the same as long as the worlds remain. But it appears that the dream of God was to create a replica of Himself, to reproduce Himself. God's multiplication is not so much a principle of multiplying two times two, but it is a principle of the increase and the reproduction of the quintessence of the Creator Himself. Not a multiplication of inanimate numbers, but reproduction of the life of God-- an increase of His light, an expansion of His knowledge, and of His power and glory.

God's command to every beast of the field and to every created thing, as well as to the man that He created in His own image, was to "be fruitful and multiply" (Genesis 1:28). "Be fruitful" came first. And then the multiplication of that fruitfulness came second. God's plan was to put into motion a never-ending eternal progression of the development of a new race. Adam was only the beginning.

> As the host of heaven cannot be counted, and the sand of the sea cannot be measured, so I will multiply the descendants of David My servant and the Levites who minister to Me.
>
> Jeremiah 33:22, NASU

Note here that the people honored by God's choice of multiplication were the descendants of the man after God's own heart (1 Samuel 13:14), and the ones dedicated to serving only the Lord. He took those with the essence of His heart and multiplied them more than any on the earth. God's principle of increase can be applied to many different circumstances: financial, material, physical, emotional, and spiritual. But the principle remains the same. What is at the heart of God's principle of increase?

> And others fell on the good soil, and yielded a crop, some a hundredfold, some sixty, and some thirty.
>
> Matthew 13:8, NASU

So many books and studies have been made of giving and prosperity that a further development of what exists is not necessary. At this point, we simply look at the subject from a somewhat different angle. As we explore increase, multiplication, and giving according to God's plan, we notice that good soil will yield, but with different levels of increase. Is the good soil referred to here the expectant soil, hopeful soil, innocent soil, or righteous soil? Often we find society lamenting the loss of innocence in its world, all the while disparaging and criticizing all those who make any kind of stand for what would be known as "righteousness."

Morality and right standing before God is immediately suspect, while innocence is touted and defiled at the same time. Various winds blow in ecclesiastical circles regarding giving and prosperity, while the world watches tongue-in-cheek for ministers to "fall from grace" and make mistakes appearing as blots upon a white cloth. And all the while, the watchers, from their critical vantage point, are living those very mistakes as a way of life. The ones who would crucify the righteous for one mistake will defend the "innocent" to the death, as long as it is an innocent from their world. It is vitally important in this season of accelerated growth and increase that we understand with revelation GOD'S principle of increase, and the increase of WHAT.

ACCELERATED GROWTH IN THE KINGDOM

As we watch new definitions of prosperity burst upon the consciousness of Kingdom dwellers, we will begin to sensitize our perceptions to watch accelerated growth in all areas of the Kingdom, using the same principles we once *expanded awareness, great expectation* taught about money. Finally we will see the realm of true multiplication on every front and every level of life. Our attention will not have to be, with apprehension and uncertainty, always on the offering totals, and the monthly giving reports. We will confidently watch, expecting great provision, because we will see it all around us: accelerated growth, expanded awareness, and great expectation.

In this season of accelerated growth and increase in the Kingdom of God, we will see the innocent and untried catapulted over the fields of temptation and into the Kingdom at an accelerated rate. Testimonies will be shorter and shorter of the hell to heaven variety where innocence was deflowered and despoiled, and then one walked through years of intimate acquaintance with the devil's workshop.

The increase of the Lord will bring man at an accelerated rate, at an expansive rate, down the corridors of experience and out into the sunlight of the knowledge of Christ. The knowledge of good and evil which brought about Adam's separation from God brought him into a knowledge of false good, and a knowledge of all of the devil's evil ways and all of the devil's acts. Man learned to visit satan in his workshop and watch him at play and at work for man's entertainment. Watching these activities of darkness have often resulted in damaging and injuring the mind, will, emotions, memories, and the habits of the body to such a degree that years are spent in cleansing, counseling and teaching about righteousness.

Accelerated Into Righteousness

Yet in this season of accelerated growth, of the multiplication of the fruitfulness of God's creation, in this season of supernatural growth, many will shoot through that middle ground of acquaintance with the devil; many will be plucked from innocence, and taken directly into the righteousness of their King.

They will be wise as serpents and harmless as doves. They will have no vengeance to overcome, no rancor, and no bitterness. They will not go through that terrible battle of mistaking man for their enemies in that middle kingdom ruled by the prince of the power of the air. They will grow into righteousness recognizing and dealing effectively with the true enemy, the god of this world: the devil and all his henchmen.

The ever-increasing light of the glory of Christ upon the faces of the righteous will be the first fruits and the first manifestation of this season of growth and expansion. The protected and innocent will meet the Lord at an early age. They will become like Jesus, the sinless spotless Lamb Who knew no sin and yet was righteous because of His Father's righteousness. The Lamb Who walked with discernment, authority, and justice in the midst of His purity.

They will become like Enoch, who first walked here, and then walked there. They will walk out of innocence into righteousness without the pain, sorrow and sighing of this world, without the veil of tears that must be rent by the crucifixion of flesh.

Puberty will no longer be a foray into rebellion and schizophrenia. It will no longer be a time of terrorizing parents and upsetting households. It will no longer be a time of total upheaval, when the mind and the body rebel against all authority. Perverse spirits will no longer rule the twelve, thirteen, and fourteen-year-olds of this world, for they will be transported into another realm, and they will walk in the Spirit. They will walk in the fullness of God's nature.

Even as the young and protected in these last days are ushered into the realm of God's righteousness, so will those who have strayed into the kingdom of darkness and become lost to light. For the Spirit of God will drag in the great harvest net and catch many unusual and unlikely fish. From all backgrounds and educations and cultures, from all levels of innocence, wariness, wiliness, and downright evil, God will make His call and receive overwhelming, unprecedented response. In this season of accelerated growth, we will see seed sown which will bear instant fruit. It will resemble more a transplanting of trees than the planting of a tiny seed.

Seed planting in the eternal realm in which God dwells bodily in all His fullness may mean a vastly different thing than seed planting as man is aware of in his time/space dimension. In God's dimension, there is no time in which to measure slow growth from a seed to a sprout to a full flower. God did not create Adam after His Seed and image as a baby. He created Adam whole and mature in His sight.

As the ages of Christendom move toward the stature of the fullness of Christ, seeds will be sown and growth accelerated to such a degree that the immaturity of yesterday will disappear as a forgotten shade before the brightness of the maturity of the present age. As surely as a nation can be born in a day (Isaiah 66:8), so will the Seed of God flower in maturity before our very eyes. And the righteousness of God will cover, cleanse, and transform, until His nature is *brightness of* born and increasing in all in the very same *maturity* miraculous multitudinous explosive growth.

IN EARTH: INCREASE OF THE NATURE OF GOD

The expansion and increase, the multiplication of our God does not refer, then, simply to a multiplication of numbers, but it refers to the expansion of the nature of our God. It is not just about Kingdom finances. It is not merely about the offering plates and the church budgets. Growth and increase in the Kingdom is ALL about the abounding, exact re-creation of His infinite creativity, wisdom, variety and joy-- His NATURE-- over and over in every situation.

We know that Jesus our Lord fed the multitudes on that long-ago mountain with the multiplication of loaves and fishes-- natural food they could recognize, ordinary food used every day. With their own eyes they saw multiplication of bread and fish. And so in these last days man will see the multiplication of ordinary things. Things he has always held in his hands as part of the tools of the survival of everyday life. But he will bless it with the blessing of his God, and see it multiplied unto thousands, and all of the wiles of the desperate wicked will attempt to come into play, like hailstones.

But the righteous in complete calm and confidence will simply bless that small remnant untouched by the wicked, and it will multiply. It will grow and expand ever-increasing, ever-enlarging. And thus man will realize that what he has seen in the multiplication of ordinary things has not just been the increase of numbers itself, but the increased ability of the dunamis power of Almighty God. Once again, He will release Himself without measure through His earthen vessels, sending out the Word of power with the ability to reproduce itself, over and over, in all the creative force of the One Who originally sent it out.

> Now He who supplies seed to the sower and bread for food, will supply and multiply your seed for sowing and increase the harvest of your righteousness.
> 2 Corinthians 9:10, NASU

Expansion of Revelation

The Word of God will enlarge, it will expand, and it will grow as bread rising from the yeast, when warmth touches it. So the Word of God will expand, as man blesses it and releases it to the nations. "But the Word of God grew and multiplied" (Acts 12:24). Revelation will grow and expand as the mind of man becomes the mind of Christ and stretches to contain the knowledge of his God.

For in this time of perpetual light, the ever-increasing and perpetual light, man will see old truths with a newness of life, with an expanded revelation. Even as the law was fulfilled in Christ and expanded and illuminated with His light but not annulled or cast away, so will man receive a revelation of giving, a revelation of the nature of God in His infinite love, creativity and wisdom.

> ...That their hearts may be encouraged, having been knit together in love, and attaining to all the wealth that comes from the full assurance of understanding, resulting in a true knowledge of God's mystery, that is,

> Christ Himself, in whom are hidden all the treasures of wisdom and knowledge.
>
> Colossians 2:2-3, NASU

And as man begins to unreservedly and unashamedly pour out of the living waters that are within him, showering the earth with the radiance of the glory of the Father of Lights, the Spirit of wisdom and understanding will burst upon the horizon. Man will begin to grasp that he has left behind the age of innocence and he has left behind the age of the knowledge of evil, and he has come into a place, a time, a realm, *an eternity of righteousness*.

Expansion, multiplication, increase, and giving, will flow out of him as the waters over a dam. It will flow out of him as the rain falls from the heavens; it will flow out of him as the steam rises from the warm and well watered earth; it will pour out of him as the fire crackles and burns exuberantly in the great bonfires of life; and it will thrust out of him like a rocket on a launching pad when the explosive energy propels it into the heavens.

WHAT GIVES BACK?

The Cry of the World

With this glorious vision of the pouring nature of God, it seems hard to believe that the cry of the world seems to be, Where is the place, where can I find something, that gives back? Does the principle really exist that actually gives back, once you have given into it? In the world, we pay the rent, and it is money that allows us to live, but there is no return. Investments which are known as a "safe" place to put your money are often not so safe, and the return meager, unsatisfying, or just downright disappointing as they seem to suck the resources worked so hard for, right out of your hands.

Even friendships or relationships can be like that. It seems to us that we give and give, and they take and take, but there never comes a return to our side of the court. In fact, the values in and of the world are so out of kilter that we often feel we exist in a state of perpetual being taken from, leeched, or stolen from; even the term "bled dry" comes to mind. And so, sadly, it is not usually in our experience that something which is given, COMES BACK.

But when we attend Christian meetings and watch Christian television, we are being assured that when we give our money, it "comes back," that what we give is multiplied, indeed that if we want to receive we must give, in order for it to come back to us. Scriptures are quoted to remind us that what we most desire, that which we need in order to support our families, will be ours if only we put the check into the offering plate. Then, and only then, is the return assured.

Many teach ardently that if we tithe, it comes back, if we give a car it comes back, if we give food, clothes, jewelry, stocks, or real estate to the Lord's people, it comes back, usually with exponential interest. Often those with only a tiny amount in their bank account or pocketbook are encouraged to clean it out and give it, in order that it "come back," a hundred-fold.

So what is the truth of this trend, this tendency, this method of raising money, this seemingly well established way of supporting Christian activities, programs, properties and all of the other legitimate and necessary vehicles that exist to propagate the gospel?

The truth is that in the Kingdom, life is not just about GIVING TO GET BACK; life is about giving, period. There is no mentality of giving to get. There is simply giving, as God gives.

GIVING: A CIRCULAR LIFE-FLOW

And so, this principle of God's multiplication, the pouring out of great increase, springs from a giving heart. In the innermost fountains of the heart of the Father is a wellspring of giving. It is a wellspring that gives without thought of the reward. He simply pours out Himself upon the earth that He has made, reproducing all that He is out of earthen vessels. As the Body of Christ, the Kingdom dwellers, pour out of the life of God within, giving without premeditation, that very power and energy which multiplies itself is released.

In the Kingdom, the word giving will no longer mean "I take what I have and with an act of my will, I hand it to you, thus meaning that I have a hole left from whence I took it." But giving will be without thought, and there will be no lack. There will be no holes; there will be life-flow instead. Just as the Father pours and the earth receives and pours back, seeding the heavens; the heavens pour and the earth receives and pours back, and it is a continual cycle, a continual life-flow of giving, so it is with the Kingdom.

The earth's life-flow of life-giving water is completely solar-driven. Without the sun the life-flow would cease immediately. The sun causes the difference in temperature moving the clouds to release the rain. The revolution of the earth on its axis around the sun delineates the seasons of the year, which control the flow of rivers and waters. It is the sun that transforms the water into vapor and causes the wind to blow vapors in from the sea. The warmth of the sun causes vapors to rise which seed the clouds with moisture, activating the flow all over again.

Multiplication, growth, and increase are all integrally a life-flow of the nature and essence of the life of God, the great Sun-Light Who made it all. We simply freely release His life, freely given to us, and watch it multiply itself, as it seeds the earth unto harvest, producing crops which pour back to Him so that the cycle can continue on its fruitful, joyous path.

life-flow of His nature

And so we will no longer calculate profit margins. We will no longer calculate percentages and cost of living raises and ten per-cent tithes, and offerings out of abundance. Instead we will open the windows of heaven within, the floodgates that will never be shut, and pour. And pour, and pour, and pour, and pour. And the thirsty earth, wherever the Lord has sent it will greedily receive and receive and receive. And as it receives, it will be instantly transformed by the glory of the Lord into yet another light-giver, another light-bearer, the candle of man lighting another candle and another candle, then another candle.

God is raising up laborers, shafts of His great light, ever-increasing and ever-multiplying their fruitfulness from this world into the next and into the next and into the next, an eternal ever-expanding, ever-growing, ever-glowing shining and radiant Garden Kingdom of Great Glory.

TEN

Thy Kingdom Come

And you shall be called the Repairer of the Breach.
Isaiah 58:12, NKJV

In the beginning God created, in His life authority and explosive power, a perfect creation pulsing with the energy of His very nature, character, and splendor. His desire to share and to give, gave birth to His most favorite creation, that of man. Man was made in God's image and likeness, and given freedom and authority to govern.

But when man began to explore his new boundaries and powers, he made the decision that has afflicted this entire complicated and interwoven cosmos ever since. God created man, and man created chaos, which then inserted itself into the perfection of God's finished work.

The closeness of God and His friend, man, suffered a painful separation. The breathtaking walks in the Eden of paradise ceased and the tangible bond of the close, loving friendship was damaged. The rapture of knowing the Beloved lay broken in pieces, and the width of the breach grew ever wider even as man began to realize what was gone.

BROKENNESS

This schism affected all of creation as the glories of God were drawn farther and farther away. And, for the time and times to come, it was irreversible. Perfection stayed with God, and man began to live with what he himself could fashion in the midst of the harsh reality of his man generated wilderness. Now, in effect, man was in one place and God was in another. There was a great expanse now existing between God and man. The distance of this separation, the vastness of this breach is almost a tangible place. Often God seems so far away, and His Word expresses this concept in the book of Isaiah.

perfection stayed with God

> For My thoughts are not your thoughts, neither are your ways My ways, says the Lord. For as the heavens are higher than the earth, so are My ways higher than your ways and My thoughts than your thoughts.
>
> Isaiah 55:8-9, AMP

As we ponder the breach, it could be likened to the expanse between earth and heaven.

It is the void between the Glory of His Presence and man's fear of nakedness.

It is the space dividing time from eternity and the gap between mankind and God's grace, mercy and love.

It is the emptiness of the human heart.

This breach is the vast barrenness of the desert places filled with powers of darkness.

It is the Distance before the pilgrim looking for the Master and the road not traveled of the dying without their Maker.

This unimaginable place is the extra untraveled mile ahead of the good Samaritan.

It is the length of the tunnel when the dying have closed their eyes and faint light glimmers in the distant darkness.

This breach was made by man and lamented by God. It separated the created from the joy of the Creator. It caused the living to live in death. It detained the development of the great dream and plan of God, Who always creates perfect and whole.

This breach is the distance of wilderness filled with nothing and empty of everything. Like a river too wide to be crossed, the breach created by man's new and selfish thoughtlessness stretches like an unending carpet of disobedience and despair. Hopeless thoughts hover and swirl: Who can repair it? Who can build a bridge, a roadway, a path back to glory?

Everything and everyone everywhere for all time were affected by this chasm. Those who are in free fall through it gasp as they realize that there is no bottom and no end. This was and is an impossible, uncrossable, unlivable situation, and man himself is to blame.

As God considered this newly made tear in the perfection of creation, what were His thoughts and emotions? How long did it take Him to perfect the plan of redemption which would save man from the consequences of his own folly? We know that the omniscient God was not surprised, and, being God, His love was continuous, His knowledge of all that was to come both immediate and complete.

But it must have been like watching a newly made massive ocean going vessel drift irrevocably away from shore, or an immense earthquake causing an island to move out of reach. What it must have been like to see the immense cosmos shifting, one thing causing another until chaos reigned instead of the brilliant garden paradise home of God.

FALLEN EARTH

And so, all through the ages, God's Life has reigned over the chaos which man made, and His power and energy continued at work even in the fallen places which seem so full of death.

Today we must look deep within the earth, this creation of the Lord God, and find the seeds of divine life hidden there. The unfathomable love of God shoots through the layers of earth like the sun through clouds after rain. His yearning sings through this fallen earth realm and everywhere that His voice is heard, death lives again.

death lives again

There are treasures of darkness hidden within the darkness of the lost and keening earth; treasures which the one dedicated to the heartbeats of the Father will search out. Put on your earth-breathing gear, O child of God, and look beyond what is seen to the veins of silver and gold hidden beneath the earth's surface. For it has not all been claimed by the evil one. All was not lost. The divine intents and purposes still sing within the molecules and atoms of this created galaxy, for what is born of God never dies. It *divine purposes* is never lost. It lives forever, and interwoven *still sing* into the very DNA of this created world remains the eternal DNA of God.

The stars sing and the firmaments declare His majesty, even as the sons of God shout for joy. This juxtaposition of light and darkness and life and death will not remain forever. The breach will not remain so. Light will triumph over darkness and Life over death, but for now, look within the darkness for the Light. Listen in the mute for the voice of the Lord and look into the blind for His Light. He who seeks, finds, and today is the day to look for the treasures of eternal life in that which is all around you. Do not dismiss what seems lost and fallen, for the wine of the Presence of Jehovah runs in its own veins, alive and vibrant with miracle working power.

You will see. You will see it. That for which your heart has longed will be revealed, for it has been there all along: the treasures found in darkness for the pleasure of the seeker; everlasting rewards for the diligent; eternal prizes for the persevering, and joy for the steadfast. Run on, O pilgrim, for your feet are made swift and your path secure by Him who leads on through the night. Watch the Light. Focus on the shining; look beneath the surface. Look for the divine changing, the fallen to the redeemed, the restored, and the transformed. God's love for His creation has never changed and now we shall comprehend it in this season of new awareness and Glory.

THE COMING OF THE KINGDOM

Heaven and earth are moving back together, and the breach is being repaired! Over the eons of time, God the Creator has recreated and redeemed, and, God-like, has used the very instrument of destruction, His man, to be His instrument of restoration. Jesus, the Restorer of the Breach, has come and transformed man into His image, that mankind might share in this great triumph of restoration, fullness and redemption.

The shadow of the Kingdom of Heaven has cast its shade upon the earth, an earnest, an inheritance, a birthright, and gradually the earth is beginning to respond.[6]

As the great Light has shined and shined, millions of hearts have been illuminated with the dream and knowledge that the kingdoms of earth are becoming the Kingdom of our Lord. Suddenly mankind has begun to hear the thundering of distant shouts. As the chorus gained in volume and passion over the ages, the great shout began to be recognized as the Voice of the Lord. The Voice of many waters, the Voice made of all of God's Kingdom dwellers, cries out across the time and space of the great Breach:

the thundering of distant shouts

Let thy Kingdom come!

Let Thy will be done in earth as it is in heaven!

Let thy Kingdom come!

And obedient to the command, this cry gained momentum and power as the Kingdom on earth grew and multiplied and began to bear fruit.

This heavenly Kingdom in earth took up the cry:

Let thy Kingdom come!

And the agreement of faith-filled believers rose across the blood strewn battlefields of the martyrs, and over the monasteries and churches and the tents of meeting, and the resounding cry continued,   Let thy Kingdom come!

And the more the persecution and the more the injustice and the more the shedding of innocent blood, the more the faith of the just rose with the passionate cry reaching the ears of the One who first sent it out. The power of agreement, the power of covenant, and the implacable, immovable strength of undeniable faith has raised the dead, moved the mountains, and changed the courses of the centuries.

The radiant countenance of the Mighty One warms and lights the weary and the battle worn, as the progress of restoration is manifested and becomes visible. Just as the pleasure of the Creator was expressed when all was finished in the beginning, surely He is expressing it once again: *IT IS GOOD*. The Breach is closing. Heaven and earth are becoming one. The Kingdom and Will of the Everlasting Father is

---

6   Mark 4:30-31

being eternally knit to His people. The majesty and splendor and joy unspeakable and full of glory are sparkling on the horizon as Truth is prevailing and the darkness is being vanquished.

There is no place of darkness in the oneness of Heaven and earth, no tears and no sorrow. Finally, the holiness and purity of the God of fire is becoming more than the lightning flashes or burning comet streaks across the firmament of earth as it was once perceived. It is now the sustaining quality of a God who tabernacles with His chosen, a God of Covenant Who has forged a city of fire to be His residency. A holy city, a city of bright light adorned as His Bride, is moving out of heaven to encompass its new dwelling places.

EVER INCREASING LIGHT

As we, the sons of God, move into maturity and union with the great Fire of all life, we are being changed from glory to glory into veritable fireballs of that same life and power and energy. The shinings of the great I Am will radiate and pulsate from the innermost being of man much like the transfiguration on the mountain when God allowed His eternal light to be perceived with the natural eyes of a mortal man, far ahead of the manifestation of the radiant ones of the Kingdom. "And He was transfigured before them; and His face shone like the sun, and His garments became as white as light" (Matthew 17:2).

> And the teachers and those who are wise shall shine like the brightness of the firmament; and those who turn many to righteousness-- to uprightness and right standing with God [shall give forth light] like the stars forever and ever.
>
> Daniel 12:3, AMP

"But let those who love Him be like the sun when it comes out in full strength" (Judges 5:31b). Have you ever sat in a massive candle lighting service when all the lights go off and a single candle starts the process? Gradually, as hundreds of candles are lit, the room begins to shine with the combined light of many vessels. Even as a cloud is made up of many particles *one large mass of brilliance* to form one visible unified form, so God's cloud of Light and Glory is made up of many members: all parts of one Body, each individual light combining to make one large mass of brilliance.

In these last days, as creation moves toward wholeness and maturity, the light of the Lamb shines from His children, the Body of Christ, the spotless and jeweled Bride. The Light that came into the world has given birth to powerhouses and lighthouses which beam into the darkness of this present age, passing the torch and carrying and multiplying the light until all the earth shall shine with His glory.

For even as one walks along the endless shores of the seas and waters of life, and the piercing call of a bird thrills the heart with its sweetness, the balm in soft winds caress the cheek and petals fall and fragrance rides along the avenues of the breath of God, so is the love of God waiting ever ready, ever joyful to reach the hungry heart.

He is the initiator, the aggressor, the wooer, the One Who reaches. And man-- man sometimes turns away, sorrowful or bitter or just empty—and sometimes man hears the knock at the door and opens that the King of Glory may come in. But always the Love and Light of God stands ever ready to fill the wasting wilderness that is man away from His God.

No sin is too heavy, no evil too thick to cover the Light, the true Light that came into the world to dispel the darkness. The people that walked in darkness HAVE SEEN, they have SEEN a great Light. And will they approach the Light or will they run away? Will they cover themselves in it, immersed, filled, sheathed, robed, and carried by the Light of the world? For this Light has a name, and His name is Jesus. He walked upon this earth and He walks it still, alive and explosive in the hearts of men, dividing the Light from the darkness and calling it DAY.

The peoples of the world have had the Daystar arise in their hearts and have given Him place, His throne resting within. Indeed they have arisen upon the face of the earth as a mighty constellation freshly created might march across the sky. They are blazing, singing, and dancing across the continents and seas, gathering momentum as they go, the power of the risen Christ growing greater and greater within them as they decrease and HE increases. The clarion call of the Ancient of Days in their ears, they advance together, with single eye and undaunted heart, sparks of joy showering abroad as they go.

The glory of the Lamb will not suddenly beam down from some hidden and exalted place upon a needy and dark world, but it will stream in fullness from all those who bear His name. It will shine with increasing purity and strength, brighter and brighter until the full day. Just as Stephen's face shone as the angels, and Moses hid his radiance with a veil, so will the sons of God manifest the radiance of His glory.

Life will be brighter than noonday and darkness will become like morning.

Job 11:17, NIV

THE MUSIC OF HOPE

Truly the music of this great advent must resound in the majestic throne rooms of the King, as the mass choirs and the heavenly instruments play the fiery music that is out of this world. The Breach is repaired! The distance is closed! The sons of God are moving into the Light! These must be the shouts of joy as heaven and earth become one. These must be the joyous refrains as thousands of years of Victory Makers rejoice in the vision.

How can we comprehend the end, lest the Omega give us revelation? He Who is the architect of this great undertaking is lending us His omniscience as we peer into another realm and gain the Revelator's vision. Come and let Me show you! He has said. Now is the time to see it. Now is the time to follow His lead, to watch and see, and to let faith arise as John of old must have experienced. Let the Lord show us that which we cannot imagine. He calls us as Kingdom dwellers to repair the Breach, even as He commanded ages ago. He is still commanding and generating and strategizing, this great General who would bring that which was torn asunder back together again.

Let His vision give us hope. Let His plan unfold at our hand. Let Him lead us and guide us as the vistas change and our bewilderment becomes expectant joy. Just as a weary traveler nearing his destination, let us catch sight of the end of this thing, which is, of course, The Beginning.

Let us see the gleaming citadel, the beacon, the signal of the end of the journey. Let us live inside ourselves the Kingdom Life which makes the visible unreal and the invisible the goal. May our minds give way to the metamorphosis necessary to live in another realm, in another day, in another dimension, even while we live here and now in this same familiar place.

Tomorrow is at hand, and with it the Kingdom of Heaven, manifesting and unfolding just as God has planned, on target, on time, and in every aspect His shining design. Hold fast that next assignment, that next step, even that next divine thought, for it is a concrete and definite step in the plan and unfolding of God as He directs us all.

JOURNEYING WITH THE KING

As we journey on in this hour of pregnant heavens and travailing earth, controlled chaos may meet our gaze. This is an hour to focus on the Person of our King, and on His authority and command. The Commander and Chief is rallying the troops for battle, and we are making ourselves ready.

It is past time for us to take our view away from the tumultuous circumstances which so bind us and lift our opening eyes to the Father's business. Our ear must be attuned to His business and His purposes, just as the child-Man Jesus did so long ago. Let us follow His example in every way as we walk out this winding and sometimes tortuous journey.

Surprising suddenlies and unexpected catastrophes do not alarm the One Whom we follow. Our soul must continually be restored and made whole with no slipping back, as we pick up the pace to keep up with the One Whom our soul loves. He is beginning to run, we realize, as we pant and attempt to watch our steps. Just step where I do, He assures us gently as we go ever more rapidly onward into unknown territory. We're going together! we realize, noticing the masses of orderly friends, neighbors, leaders and disciples journeying with us. They are running alongside! We are aligned together, just look at the order!

We're actually not watching one another, but each is watching the King, following His orders and going in the path He sets before us. But it makes sense! we cry. There is a pattern, and with each in his place, the formations move as one, taking the territory and keeping the timetable intact. It's a miracle! Truly, the mustard seeds of our faith keep us in line as the mountains of difficulty and impossibility disappear before our eyes. This is a Kingdom journey! We have come together! At last we are aligning with Him, with one another and with His great plan.

The Kingdom and the King are on the move! This is the hour to move as well. Let us make all of the necessary changes. Let us repent and forgive and love again! Let the past flow away, the current of the future carrying it far from our remembrance. Let faith arise, hope expand and strength grow. Let the Husbandman prune our branches, that our fruit may be full and sweet and refreshing. The paradise of Eden looms once again in our vision, and the hastening pace quickens our heart. The dead will live again!

The Kingdom of Heaven is at hand!
Thy Kingdom come and Thy will be done
In earth as it is in heaven!   Amen!

OTHER BOOKS BY LORA ALLISON

Flaming Purpose
Lora Allison's story is filled with fires, floods, and mighty testimonies of the delivering and healing power of our risen Savior. Written in a readably warm and humorous style, this book also contains revelatory teaching on the fire of God.

Stress Relief: Reflections for Saturday Mornings
This is a devotional book designed to be read in those wonderful mornings with the Lord. It contains real life stories of pleasure, treasure, and testing, and will bring refreshing and strength for the week ahead.

Overcomer: The Emerging Church of the Third Day
Teaching with a fresh perspective on the Overcoming heart enlightens those who long for God's eternal Light, Truth, and Holiness. Prophetic words to the Body of Christ encourage and strengthen.

Celebration
A practical and scriptural look at worship released visually, with how-to's, diagrams, and 59 glorious color photographs. Gift-book quality.

The Importance of Covering
Designed to be a Quick Read, this is a vital and practical look at the often controversial subject of spiritual covering.

For more information about Celebration International Ministries and to visit our online store of books, teaching CD's, DVD's and other materials, we invite you to visit our website!

www.celebrationministries.com